MANX SLAVE TRADERS

Other titles by the same author

In print
The Isle of Man in Smuggling History
Scottish Customs & Excise Records
Strathclyde's Smuggling Story
Dumfries & Galloway's Smuggling Story
Family Histories in Scottish Customs Records
The Smuggling Story of Two Firths
George Moore & Friends
The Smuggling Story of the Northern Shores

with John Gibson-Forty: *The Nimrod Work-Related Stress Manual*

In preparation
The Running Trade
Walter Lutwidge, merchant of Whitehaven

with Eric Graham: *Robert Arthur, merchant in Irvine*

MANX
SLAVE TRADERS

A Social History
of the Isle of Man's involvement in the Atlantic Slave Trade

Frances Wilkins BA

Published by:
Wyre Forest Press
8 Mill Close, Blakedown, Kidderminster, Worcestershire DY10 3NQ

Printed by:
Redwood Books Limited
Kennet Way, Trowbridge, Wiltshire BA14 8RN

ISBN 1 897725 13 2

Contents

Page

Illustrations

Tables

Sources of Illustrations and Acknowledgements

Sources

Figures 1.1, 1.2, 3.2 & 4.1 from the Ingates and Outgates [MNHL 10058 Ingates and Outgates for 1718, 1761 and 1750]

Figures 2.1, 4.3 and 6.2 from Robert Morden's Maps reproduced in the 1695 edition of *Camden's Britannica*

Figures 3.1 from a photograph held by the Manx National Heritage

Figure 4.2 from Nicholas Visscher *Anglica Regnum* 1690

Figure 5.1 from a miniature held by the Manx National Heritage

Figures 5.2, 5.3, 5.4 & 6.3 from the Atholl papers [MNHL 9707 APX69(2nd)-28(a), APX69(2nd)-14, APX46-26 & AP52-4]

Figure 6.1 from Murdoch Mackenzie (the elder) *The Isle of Man* 1775

Figure 6.4 from the Bridge House papers [MNHL BH3522]

Figures 7.1, 8.2 and 8.3 from the Encyclopaedia Britannica 1st edition 1771

Figures 8.1, 8.4 and 9.1 (and his signature) from the Memoirs of the Late Captain Hugh Crow of Liverpool

Figure 10.1 based on *A New and Correct Map of the Coast of Africa from Cape Blanco to the Coast of Angola*: 1746

Signatures of John Murrey, William Teare, Paul Bridson, Mary Reeves, George Moore, Hugh Cosnahan, Ambrose Lace and John Corran from assorted will documents. Signatures on p1 and Robert Kennedy signature from Atholl Papers [MNHL 9707 AP40B-6 & AP44B-28] Charles Christian signature from MNHL 9381

Acknowledgements

Figures 1.1, 1.2, 3.1, 3.2, 4.1, 5.1, 5.2, 5.3, 5.4, 6.3 & 6.4 and the signatures reproduced by courtesy of Manx National Heritage

Figures 4.2 and 6.1 reproduced by courtesy of Martin Moore

Ambrose Lace's signature reproduced by courtesy of the Lancashire Record Office

Acknowledgements

My very grateful thanks are due to the staff of the Manx National Heritage library in Douglas for all their patient assistance during the research necessary for this book - and particularly for help with the photocopies of innumerable wills of 'drowned mariners'.

I would like to thank staff at the University of Birmingham library, University of Essex Data Archive Service, University of Keele Information Services – library, University of Leicester library, Merseyside Maritime Museum, Cumbria Record Office (Carlisle and Whitehaven), Denbighshire Record Office, Lancashire Record Office (Preston), Liverpool Record Office, Carnegie Library, Ayr, Birmingham City Library and Derby Museum and Art Galleries.

Also thanks are due to all those on the Isle of Man who supplied essential background information and support: Frank Cowin, Martin Moore, Ray Moore, Chris Pickard and Angela Rogers.

Special thanks are due to David Richardson, Steve Behrendt and Melinda Elder for sharing their information about the slave trade; to Robert Hasell-McCosh for access to the Dalemain Archive; to Eric Graham for help with Scottish vessels and to Roger Nixon for all his painstaking work at PRO, Kew.

Finally I would like to thank my son, Steven, for his technical assistance and my husband, Dennis, for putting up with my frequent absences on the Island, and for all his support.

INTRODUCTION

The eighteenth century English government were well-aware that East Indian cloths and other goods for the slave trade were warehoused on the Isle of Man and collected by the Liverpool vessels on their outward voyages. They attempted to protect the East India Company's monopoly by passing Acts which banned the importation of these goods into the Channel Islands, and Man. To enforce this, from time to time revenue cruisers attempted to stop vessels either transporting the goods to the Island, or after they had unloaded their cargo. On one occasion three of these vessels were seized by a customs officer at Liverpool, their next port of call. The Board of Customs for Scotland, which now included Basil Cochrane, a former Governor of the Isle of Man, reported to the Treasury in 1764 about the continued existence of these warehouses.

There is recent information about the links between the Isle of Man and Liverpool during the slave trade period. Any vessel trading from Britain to the West Indies or America was required to have a Plantation register. The results of research by Maurice Schofield and Chris Pickard into the Manx merchants listed in the Liverpool plantation registers was incorporated in the *Liverpool Trade and Shipping 1744 to 1786* database. Hugh Thomas in *The Slave Trade* noted the existence of the Isle of Man as one of the factors why the total number of Guinea vessels sailing from Liverpool increased after 1740.

The most famous description of a Manx captain in the slave trade was the *Memoirs of the Late Captain Crow*, published in 1830. Many articles about Crow have appeared in such publications as *The Mariner's Mirror* and *Manx Millennium 2000 AD*. A.W. Moore in his *Manx Worthies* dated 1901 included a section on 'Slave-traders' under 'The Merchant Service'. Apart from Crow he listed as 'more especially slavers' Ambrose Lace, Christian, William Crow, Edward Clarke, Shimmin and John Clague. In his paper on *Slave Trade Captains* Stephen Behrendt identified twenty-eight Manx captains sailing from Liverpool between 1770 and 1807.

To date no detailed study has been made of the Manx involvement in the Atlantic Slave Trade per se. The current research developed out of an apparently different project – on the running trade. In 1813 the Duke of Atholl referred to John Taubman 'whose extensive smuggling transactions were the principal means of my family being deprived of their rights in the Island'. Taubman had at the time of the Revestment Act in 1765 'a great quantity of spirits, teas, wines etc deposited in the Island for the purpose of smuggling to England'. To estimate Taubman's true role in the chain of events which resulted in the Crown purchasing the fiscal rights of the Isle of Man from the Duke of Atholl, the Douglas customs entries from 1761 to 1764 were searched for tea importations. The result was unexpected: not only was Taubman merely one of many merchants with tea ventures on the Rotterdam vessels calling at Douglas but other goods of great value were also on board. These goods included East Indian textiles, beads, brass pans, looking glasses, knives, cutlasses, guns, pistols, gunpowder, iron bars, spread eagle dollars and cowrie shells. They could have had only one outlet: the 'Guinea trade'.

The next stage was to establish how many Manx merchants were involved in importing these goods – did they also own any of the slaving vessels sailing to the Guinea coast of Africa? How many other Manx captains, like Hugh Crow, and his brother William and David Christian mentioned in his *Memoirs*, were in the slave trade? Were there Manx surgeons on the Guinea vessels and how many of the crews were Manxmen?

An initial picture of the Manx role in the Atlantic slave trade was presented at a day school in Douglas during October 1998. The subject raised so much interest that further research was undertaken - both on the Island and at several locations in England. The range of these locations is indicated both in the Acknowledgements and the section on Source Material. The significant fact is that all these records refer to the Island's role in the Atlantic slave trade.

This book is the outcome of that additional research. A particular feature of the book is that it is based almost entirely on documents written at the time. This has both advantages and disadvantages. On the one hand it ensures authenticity without the accumulated layers of hearsay and legend which tend to embellish stories of the past, and of the slave trade in particular. On the other hand the surviving records are only a tiny fraction of what was written, and the story has to be told as a mosaic of fragments gained from separate and often unrelated sources.

The material thus selects itself in the sense that one can only use what has survived. For this book it has been further selected to include only information with a clear Manx interest. A judgement has had to be made as to who were the Manxmen, and which the Manx-related ships and how substantial was the Manx component of the many joint ventures with English merchants. These criteria have been made broad rather than narrow in the interests of telling a coherent narrative.

At the same time the whole venture of writing this book started because of the very extensive Manx records still surviving on the Island, so that a wide range of relevant material was available right from the start. This was subsequently expanded by searching for references to Manx activities in maritime archives held elsewhere – in record offices, libraries and private collections.

Perhaps the most surprising finding has been the omnipresence of the Manx influence be it in the letter of instruction to a Liverpool captain, telling him to call at Douglas and apply to a named merchant there to complete his cargo of Guinea goods, or in the names found on a crew list of a slaving vessel.

In terms of the Isle of Man's eighteenth century activities, it is important to put the slave trade into its proper context. The First Edition of the Encyclopædia Britannica, published in 1771, defined a slave as:

'*A person in the absolute power of a master, either by war or contest. We find no mention of slaves before the deluge; but immediately after, viz. In the curse of Canaan: whence it is easily inferred that servitude increased soon after that time; for in Abraham's time we find it generally established ... Slavery is absolutely abolished in Britain and France, as to personal servitude. Slaves make a considerable article of traffic in America*'.

As an article of trade, every care was taken to deliver the slaves to the markets in the West Indies and America in as good a condition as possible – herein lay the profits of a slaving venture. Some of the slave traders were used to trading in human beings – they also shipped convicts. To captains like Hugh Crow a far worse problem was the inhumane treatment of 'volunteers' by the navy's press gangs, on land and at sea.

The second half of the eighteenth and the early nineteenth centuries witnessed a major expansion in the overseas trade of the regions round the Irish Sea. By 1752 Liverpool was well on the way to becoming the major English port in the Atlantic slave trade, relegating Bristol and London to second and third places respectively.

Although the slave trade is always referred to as having been 'triangular' this was not in fact true. Many of the goods which formed the west African cargoes were not from England – they came from the East Indies, by way of the East India Companies. As a result there was an additional side to the triangle – that of obtaining these cargoes for the slaving vessels. It was inevitable that the Isle of Man by virtue both of its location and, until 1765, its peculiar financial status, should play a role in the Liverpool trade, if simply as a source of the cheaper Dutch East India goods. That the Island's role became so important is a tribute to the trading acumen of the people who lived there.

The term 'slave trade' was not in common use during the eighteenth century. Instead it was frequently referred to as the 'Guinea' or 'African' trade. The vessels were known as the Liverpoolian Guineamen and mariners lost over several hundreds of miles of the African coast were said to have died 'on the Guinea coast'. As a result the term 'Guinea' is used throughout the book when referring to the Atlantic slave trade.

It should be emphasised that it is not a book about the Guinea trade in general – several books already exist on this subject. It is about the Isle of Man's involvement in that trade. As a result it tells a somewhat distorted story - that of the sections of the trade in which the Island took part. The outward cargoes are described in terms of what was available in the Isle of Man; the triangular trade is portrayed through the experiences of Manx slave captains, surgeons and mariners who were there, and of Manx-related vessels; the homeward cargoes discussed are those that were landed on the Island.

Gomer Williams [*History of the Liverpool Privateers with an account of the Liverpool Slave Trade*] includes invaluable information about the Guinea trade – and quotations that are appropriate to the Isle of Man. These have not been transcribed in detail here – copies of the book are still available. Exceptions are the letter of instruction to Ambrose Lace as captain of the *Marquis of Granby* and the letters from Old Calabar to Lace.

Similarly large extracts from Hugh Crow's *Memoir* have been reproduced frequently – and a facsimile of his book is in print. Again some limited use has been made of this material. Crow's comments often provide extra detail in illustrating a particular point. Two examples of this are impressment by the navy of the crews on board the Guinea vessels and Crow's experiences when imprisoned in France.

The contemporary records create their own problems. Often a decision has had to be made about which spelling of a surname is more appropriate: Finch instead of Vinch, Murray for Murrey, Kneal for Kneale, Teare for Tear etc. Where possible other spellings have been standardised. The eighteenth century quotations have been re-punctuated to aid ease of reading the text. Similarly the multiple use of the words 'and', 'that' and 'said' have been omitted, unless this changes the meaning of the passage. The sources of the quotations and other information, where appropriate, are noted and listed in the section on Source Material. Remarks in square brackets [] are added by the author.

The book is divided into two sections: On the Isle of Man and Off the Isle of Man. The first section looks at the beginnings of the Manx involvement in the slave trade in 1718 and traces the development of the Island as a main source of Guinea goods. Then the Revestment Act changed the pattern completely – the goods could no longer be warehoused there and the slave trade merchants who had previously lodged their cargoes on the Isle of Man were forced to look elsewhere. The second section concentrates on the rise of the Manx mariners, who appear to have increased considerably in numbers post Revestment.

Each chapter is told from the viewpoint of a particular individual – their signature appears below the title heading. This approach has been used to emphasise the social history aspect of the book. Who was the first merchant to import Guinea goods into the Island? John Murray; who was the main mover against the proposed bridge over Douglas harbour and for the enlargement of Peel harbour? George Moore; who gave evidence about the massacre at Old Calabar to the Parliamentary Enquiry into the slave trade? Ambrose Lace.

Two documents and a book which surfaced during this research have been used in three chapters in the Off the Island section. The first of these is a log of part of the voyage of the *Ranger*, of which John Corran was captain. The crew list for the *Ranger* exists as a Liverpool muster roll and there are copies of Corran's will both on the Island and at the Lancashire Record Office. These all help to 'put flesh on the bones' of the document, which is valuable in its own right, as it gives intimate details of the daily events on board a Guinea vessel.

The second is a somewhat strange document written by Charles Christian, brother of Fletcher Christian of mutiny on the *Bounty* fame. This document does not relate directly to the slave trade – but it does include details of a Guinea voyage when Christian was surgeon on board the *William*, sailing from Liverpool in February 1799. Again a muster roll exists with crew names and this confirms some of the comments in the Christian account, particularly about the numbers impressed at Jamaica. The chance mention of the existence of this document at a dinner party emphasises the somewhat hit and miss approach that is inevitable when attempting to collect material from a wide range of unpublished sources.

Finally the published journal of John Newton's voyage in the *Duke of Argyle* in 1750 also includes a daily account of what was happening on board the vessel – and in the surrounding area. This is of value here because a Manxman, John Bridson, was chief mate. From the entries in the journal it has been possible to build a picture of Bridson's duties – and his death. The journal also solved the mystery of Edward Lawson who was recorded on the Island as having died on the Guinea coast 'about 18 years ago'. He did indeed die there - following a trip by the *Duke of Argyle*'s longboat, when Bridson was in charge.

The Appendices attempt to emphasise the sheer magnitude of the Island's involvement in the slave trade. Appendix 1 is a calendar of events from 1700 to 1830, only recording those which were Manx-related – it covers six pages. It also acts as a supplement to and summary of information found elsewhere in the book. Appendix 2 lists 90 Guinea vessels which are believed to have called at the Island. In the majority of cases there is evidence from at least one source that the vessels were there: to collect part of their Guinea cargoes en route for Africa or to unload some of their rum etc on their way back to their home ports. Where a reference has been found to 'three Guinea ships riding in Peel Bay' or six vessels waiting in Liverpool to collect gunpowder on the Island then an attempt has been made to put names to them – and to assess their Manx links.

Appendix 3 serves to avoid clogging the text with too much detailed information about the East Indian cloths and other Guinea goods available on the Island between 1718 and 1764. It lists several of the different cloths which appear in the customs entries, together with the variations of their spellings, and it describes some of these cloths. It also gives details of cargoes of Guinea goods on Dutch vessels and the contents of trunks of East Indian cloths imported from Liverpool.

In the absence of later information, Appendix 4 only includes the Manx partners in Guinea vessels between 1744 and 1786. Appendix 5 records Manx mariners who died 'on the Guinea coast'. Most of this information comes from the microfilms of wills held at the Manx National Heritage library – these together with other sources produced over 300 names of mariners who appear to have died in the Guinea trade. Finally Appendix 6 gives details of Ambrose Lace's voyages as a Guinea captain.

The Source Material section explains how this intricate picture of Manx involvement in the Guinea trade has been developed.

This book is dedicated to Patricia, Lady Daunt

On the Isle of Man

In May 1764 the Commissioners of His Majesty's Treasury requested the Board of Customs in Edinburgh to make a 'most strict enquiry into the smuggling trade carried on between the Isle of Man and Scotland'. The response, dated 7 June 1764, said:

'That in the course of the enquiries which have been made on this occasion information has been received that large warehouses are established in the Island of Man and well furnished with such articles of commerce as are necessary for the trade on the coast of Africa, and that the ships fitted out from Britain for the coast do touch at the Island and receive such goods on board as may be proper for completing the assortment of their cargoes'.[1]

This document was signed by the four Commissioners for the Board of Customs for Scotland. Between 1751 and 1761 Basil Cochrane had been Governor of the Isle of Man so that he was be in a strong position to give detailed information to the Enquiry. His signature appears frequently throughout the Manx records.

Figure 1.1: Extracts from the Ingates for Ramsey 25th August 1718

Ingates
25th Augt 1718

Mr Murray orders of board the Goodspeed
Arthur Smith master from Rotterdam five
Casques of Beads 2 boxes of Beads called —
Rangoos six Chests of old sheets six Chests of
course stuff for Guinnea val: of the above goods
as appeard by bill of parcells from Rotterdam
is 316..15..0 allowing 11 guildrs for a pound
sterling - - - - - - - 7..18..4½   10   10 . 4½

In the sd Chests among the stuff was } 1..13..1
400 yds of Callicos - - - -

one Casque Neptunes with Brass } 0..7..0
paints qt 700 lb

5 Keggs of Gunpowder qt 700 lb - 0..11..8

Lod

Mr Murray orders of board the Charity Simon
Williamson master six Chests of Guinnea stuff
& Callicos val: of the stuff by bill of parcells
is 180 - - - - - - - 4..10..0

In the sd Chests 1026 yds Callicos - 4..5..0

4 halfs Casques of Neptunes with one } 0..19..0
brass paints qt 19 hund: wt -

20 Chests of old sheets are 133 - 3..6..6   18 . 18 . 10

60 Barrells of Gunpowder qt 60 hund } 5..0..0
wt - - - - - -

5 Tonn ½ of Iron - - - - 0 . 18..4

1

The Guinea Cargoes

John Murray (signature)

In August 1718 the *Goodspeed*, Arthur Smith master, and the *Charity*, Simon Williamson, arrived at Ramsey from Rotterdam. John Murray of Douglas landed goods from both vessels. These goods included five casks, two boxes and forty-eight chests of beads, old sheets and coarse stuffs 'for Guinea' (see Figure 1.1). The amount of detail included in the Ingates suggests that this was an early, if not the first, entry of Guinea goods on the Island.

The invoices were in Dutch currency and the value of the goods was calculated by allowing 11 guilders for a pound British: total £629 15s. An approximate conversion is to multiply eighteenth century currency by 50 to get 20th century values[2] i.e. the goods were worth about £30,000. [Values quoted throughout this book are in 18th century £ sterling – or in Manx or Irish currency, as indicated]. The value of the goods was needed for the calculation of duty. This was at the rate of 6d in the pound sterling i.e. £12 8s 4½d on £629 15s.

Beads, old sheets and coarse stuffs

The beads were described as 'rangoes'. These were arrangoes – red carnelian from India. Beads formed a major part of the Guinea cargoes. In November 1764 William Davenport, a Liverpool merchant, instructed his captain William Patten of the *William*, to collect a selection of beads from Hugh Cosnahan of Douglas. These included:

30 bunches small white beads, 30 bunches small blue do., 20 bunches small yellow do., 20 bunches small green do. and 120 bunches large red pocado.[3]

In March that year Cosnahan had imported from Rotterdam on the *Neptune*, John Kelly master, beads of the same value.

The beads were primarily to exchange for slaves but they also had other uses. Captain Hugh Crow commented that they were 'distributed amongst the women [slaves] to amuse them' on the Middle Passage from Africa to the West Indies.[4]

The old sheets and coarse stuffs would have come directly from Holland. The old sheets, literally second-hand ones that had been used as bed linen, would be dyed locally in west Africa and used for loincloths. Dyestuffs, such as indigo from Holland, camwood from Africa and logwood from America were available on the Isle of Man. It is not clear whether any actual dyeing of Guinea goods took place there or whether the indigo in particular was exported as part of a Guinea cargo. Between 1718 and 1764 over 7,000 of these old sheets were landed on the Island.

The stuffs were coarse woollen fabric manufactured in Holland specifically for the Guinea trade. There is some evidence that the Isle of Man attempted to provide home-produced 'stuffs'. In the early years of the slave trade vessels would clear out for 'the Maderas' rather than Africa.[5] [The reason for this is unclear]. In April 1721 Christopher Bridson loaded 300 yards of frize at Derbyhaven on the *Oak*, himself captain, for Madeira. This was followed in December that year by Henry Moore, Phil Moore, Robert Moore and Mr Murray who loaded at Douglas 1,476 yards of flaxen cloth, 1,983 yards of frize and 2,232½ yards of 'Hewersden' cloth on the *Betty*, John James captain, also for Madeira (see Appendix 2.1).

East Indian Cloths

There were 1,420 yards of calico in the Murray cargoes. These were listed separately because they carried a duty of 1d per yard i.e. £5 18s 4d. Between 1718 and 1764 over 25,700 yards of calico were imported into the Island, bringing in a duty in excess of £100. Calico appears to have been isolated from the other cloths because various Acts of Parliament had been passed prohibiting the importation and wearing of it. In 1720 calico was described as 'a kind of linen manufacture made of cotton, chiefly in the East Indies, some of which are painted with various flowers of different colours; others that are never dyed, having a stripe of gold and silver quite through the piece; and at each end they fix a tissue of gold, silver and silk, intermixed with flowers'. The wearing of calico in Britain had become 'a general grievance and occasioning unspeakable distress upon our own manufactures'.[6] It was also an important item in the Guinea cargoes. Although chintz was basically painted or stained calico, it did not pay the duty of 1d per yard. Over 5,200 pieces of chintz were imported during the this period.

Calico was the only East Indian cloth in the Murray cargoes but a much wider range of such textiles was available on the Island. These formed a major part of the Guinea cargoes. The bulk of the cloth was in the form of cottons of different varieties. These included the coarse bafts, the medium grade seersuckers and ginghams and the fine muslins. There are severe problems when attempting to identify some of the cloths listed in the Manx records: they were known in the East Indies by local names – and these names suffered in their translation first into Dutch invoices and then into the customs entries on the Island (see Appendix 3.1and 3.2).

Similarly it is almost impossible to assess the total volume of cloth imported into the Island as it was often referred to not in yards but in numbers of 'pieces'. A piece has been described as 'about 5 metres in length'[7] although there is evidence in the Manx customs entries that these pieces actually varied from 5 to 20 yards. Yet the pieces were used as a currency in west Africa – a slave would be worth so many pieces. Based on his experiences as captain of the *Marlborough* at Whydah in 1759, Ambrose Lace gave an 'aide memoir' to the next captain of the vessel, William Benson. This listed the customs, which had to be paid to the King of Dahomey before a ship could make her 'whole trade'. These customs were equivalent to the goods that would have purchased eighteen slaves. Lace defined the value of a slave as 10 long cloths or 10 blue bafts or 10 patten (sic) chintz – see below.[8]

Finally the customs entries intermingle pieces of a particular material, for example annabasses [another name for fustian, or cotton stuff] with actual garments: lungees [longees], which were used in India as loin cloths, romals [neckerchiefs] and handkerchiefs. To confuse the situation even further these garments could be made of cotton or silk, which was also known as herba.

Often the value of a cargo included a range of cloths, beads etc. so that it is difficult to identify the cost of the individual items. There are exceptions. A detailed list has survived, which was used to calculate the duty owed by Pat Savage on a trunk of goods imported on the *William & Anne*, Oliver Garner master, from Liverpool in 1737. The values quoted per piece are: cotton romals 6s, bandanoes 14s, seersuckers 14s, longee romals 16s, persians [taffeta] 16s 6d and damask £4.[9]

Gunpowder, neptunes and iron bars

John Murray's 1718 cargoes also included 60 barrels and five kegs of gunpowder, one full cask and four half casks of neptunes 'viz. brass pans', and 5½ tons of iron. Values were not given for these goods because the duties were calculated per hundred weight at 1s 8d for gunpowder, 1s for neptunes and 2d for iron. During the first half of the eighteenth century there was a gradual change-over as the hundredweight became 112 lbs instead of 100 lbs. This complication makes it difficult to estimate the exact weights of these articles imported into the Island. There is also evidence that the deputy searchers at the ports, and their junior customs officers, often used different measures, even between the initial entry of goods from a vessel [i.e. the cargo according to the invoice and the merchant's declaration] and the post entry [i.e. when the cargo had been unloaded and the exact amount measured].

As a result all the values quoted in this book for imports of Guinea goods only include the beads, cloths etc and exclude the gunpowder, neptunes and iron. This means that the figures are an underestimate. Analyses have been made of the composition of the goods imported by individual merchants, however, and there is no evidence to suggest that the missing items would change their relative importance in Table 2.1.

Between 1718 and 1764 some 4,650 barrels, 300 kegs and 265 casks of gunpowder, weighing over 3,965 hundred weight [reckoning at 100 lbs per cwt] were landed on the Island. This gunpowder was a constant fire hazard on board the Guinea ships. William Crow, Hugh Crow's brother, was chief mate on board the *Othello*, David Christian captain, when she caught fire at Bonny on the African coast. Crow describes the incident: 'before any thing effectual could be done to extinguish the flames, she suddenly blew up, and of several whites, and about one hundred and twenty blacks, who were on board, a few only escaped destruction'. Christian and Crow 'had scarcely left the vessel when the awful explosion took place'.[4] Hugh Crow was offered the post of mate on Christian's next command, the *Parr*, 'but had cause to change my mind'.[4] The *Parr* blew up at Bonny in 1798 and this time Christian died.

Neptunes were large brass pans used in west Africa for processing palm oil and salt. According to Hugh Crow, the Brass tribe derived their name from the importations 'of a kind of European-made brass pans' which they supplied to the interior 'from the earliest times on record. The article is now largely imported from Liverpool, both to Bonny and Calabar'.[4] A section of the Niger delta is still known as Brass.

Crow described various uses for palm oil: 'We frequently bought from the natives considerable quantities of dried shrimps to make broth; and a very excellent dish they made when mixed with flour and palm oil, and seasoned with pepper and salt. Both whites and blacks were fond of this mess'. It also helped to keep the slaves occupied on the Middle Passage: 'About eleven, if the day were fine, they washed their bodies all over, and after wiping themselves dry were allowed to use palm oil, their favourite cosmetic'.[4]

In 1802 Charles Kneal, captain of the *Lottery*, was instructed to barter his 'well assorted cargo' at Bonny for 290 negroes. 'Besides which we expect you will be able to procure a quantity of palm oil, which you will take especial care to put into puncheons well iron-hooped'.[10]

The iron bars would have been about 9 inches long, weighing 20 lbs each. Once they reached west Africa these would be manufactured into hoe blades or machetes, and sometimes spears or arrowheads.[11] Between 1718 and 1764 over 41,500 of these bars were imported into the Island.

Guinea Goods on the Island

The Murray cargoes give a good indication of the types of Guinea goods that were landed on the Island. Table 1.1 lists the total range available. Other items on this list that are worthy of note include tobacco and alcohol, cowries, spread eagle dollars, looking glasses and provisions. Some of these were not just for exchange. Crow mentioned that 'pipes and tobacco were then supplied to the men [slaves]' during the Middle Passage.[4]

Table 1.1: Guinea Goods Available on the Isle of Man 1718 to 1764

East Indian cloths, coarse stuffs, knittings	beads (both glass & stone), amber & coral
old sheets, silesias or platillos (coarse linen)	looking glasses, hats, fans, combs, canes
guns, muskets & pistols, stock locks & flints	bells, hawk bells, horse bells
gunpowder	chinaware, earthenware & drinking glasses
axes, cutlasses, knives	cowrie shells
iron bars, wrought & manufactured iron	spread eagle dollars
brass pans (neptunes), kettles & rods	stockfish, ling fish, herrings
copper kettles, bars & rods; pewter basins	arrack, wine, brandy, spirits, ale & spa water
empty glass bottles, guardvins & cases	tobacco pipes, tobacco, snuff

Because of the large quantities of goods passing through the Isle of Man as part of the running trade, it is impossible to identify with any degree of accuracy what proportion of either tobacco or alcohol went into the Guinea cargoes.

The Davenport instructions to Captain Patten mentioned above also included 3 dozen [bottles] of claret.[3] George Moore of Peel attempted to attract the Liverpool vessels to his port by importing the correct type of brandy for a Guinea cargo. In February 1758 he offered Bordeaux brandy 'suitable for particular markets' to Haliday & Dunbar of Liverpool 'or any of your friends for the African coast'. As he explained to them 'I must own that the brandy I lately imported was calculated to serve my inclination of encouraging your Guinea merchants who deal in that commodity to call here'.[12] Moore's agent in Bordeaux, George Ainslie, had also purchased a cargo of brandy in Spain and Moore was proud to offer both varieties to Thomas Rumbold & Co, owners of the *Hare*, George Colley captain.[13] There is no direct evidence that Moore was successful in this venture or that the Guinea vessels began to call at Peel regularly for brandy.

In 1744 Robert Murray, William Murray senior's brother, was apparently supplying the slave trade with ale imported from Ireland. On 26 December he landed from the *Vernon*, Jeffrey Mashiter master, one hundred dozen bottles containing ten barrels of ale. He was bound 'in the sum of fifty pounds to his Grace's use' that this ale would be 'reshipped off this Isle within two months'.[14] As there are no Outgates for this period, it is impossible to know where the ale went.

The <u>cowrie shells</u> were imported into Holland from the Maldive Islands off south-west India. Those imported into the Island filled over 2,000 casks, 235 chests, 300 cases and 45 barrels, which considering their small size implies enormous numbers. Once in Africa these shells were used as currency. They were strung in 40s, which were known as 'tokees'. Five strings of these were called a gallina [the local name for a chicken] and 100 tokees were worth a 'cabess' [an iron bar].[8]

Lace continued his aide memoir to Benson by stating what happened on the African coast after the customs had been agreed. The Vice Roy would give the captain nine servants, each of whom had to be paid on a regular basis. One of these was the 'conducter' whose duty was 'to take care of the goods that comes and goes to and from the waterside which you deliver him in count and he's obliged to answer for things delivered him'. He had to be paid '2 gallinas of cowries every time he conducts any thing whether coming or going and one flask of brandy every Sunday'. There were also fixed prices for each load of goods carried from the ship to the shore, to pay for the slaves: 'You pay 3 tokees of cowries for every load such as one anker [cask of spirits], 40 Sililees [Silesias], 10 pieces cloth and so in proportion for small goods but when loads are very heavy you pay more as ten gallinas for a chest'.[8]

The silver <u>spread eagle dollars</u> were also imported in large quantities - over 60 bags, casks and boxes containing at least 26,450 coins. The earliest date found for the importation of these dollars is 1741. Maria Theresa became archduchess of Austria after her father's death on 20 October 1740 and it is supposed that these were Maria Theresa spread eagles.

Looking glasses were a major item. Twelve chests, five boxes, 20 cases and 6 casks of these have been identified in the entries. Gomer Williams quotes a letter from Grandy King George at Old Town, Old Calabar to Ambrose Lace, listing items which he was to send by any of his vessels. These included for the King himself a looking glass, which was to be six foot long and six foot wide – 'Let it have a strong wooden frame'.[8]

Finally there were the provisions for the crew, both on the outward voyage and during the prolonged stay on the African coast, and the 'necessaries' for the vessel. Dried stockfish and lingfish came in bundles and hoops as part of the Guinea cargoes from Rotterdam. In September 1729 Manx potatoes were exported for Madeira on the *Hannah*, Thomas Bennett captain (see Appendix 2.1). Vinegar was needed to sprinkle on the deck and 'keep the ship sweet'. Tallow from Ireland was used for making candles and to smear on the hull as a guard against shipworm.

The Guinea Cargoes
When considering the wide variety of goods available on the Isle of Man for the Guinea trade, it is important to remember the destination of these items: the west coast of Africa. The suppliers of the slaves were only interested in an exchange that gave them items either not available locally or of a superior quality. Prestige was an all-important factor. In other words the African market dictated the cargoes of the Guinea vessels, and therefore the goods that were landed on the Island.

Most of these goods could not be supplied in England at this stage. The Guinea merchants had to purchase their cargoes through the East India Company in London. Prices were high – as were the duties that had to be paid. All this added to the costs of the voyage. Any savings that could be made in the purchase of the goods was therefore worthy of consideration. The Isle of Man was an interesting alternative source of goods: they would cost less and the duties were lower.

Murray was not the only merchant involved in the cargoes delivered at Ramsey. Robert Moore, also based in Douglas, had landed one chest of beads, two chests of old sheets and three chests of coarse stuffs for Guinea valued at £140 18s plus 180 yards of calico, a cask of neptunes and 14 kegs and one barrel of gunpowder from the *Goodspeed*.

It appears that these goods were repacked. Some of them only stayed on the Island for a few hours (see Figure 1.2). They were exported by John Murray on the *Scipio*, Captain Trafford and on the *Success Galley*, Thomas Moister. There is evidence of the *Scipio* at Liverpool. On 12 August 1718 Richard Gildart loaded pewter, copper, brass manufactures, wrought iron, tobacco pipes, earthenware, shot and glass beads on board for Madeira.[15] The *Success* has not been identified but Thomas Tarleton's vessel the *Tarleton* – no master's name given - left Liverpool on 23 August 1718 for Madeira with gunpowder, glass bottles, pewter and wrought iron on board.[15] Robert Moore put goods on the *Peace Galley*, Cheatwood Pride commander, also for Madeira. On 14 August 1718 Foster Cunliffe had loaded wrought iron and copper manufactures on the *Peace* at Liverpool.[15]

Figure 1.2: Extract from the Ramsey Outgates for 25 August 1718

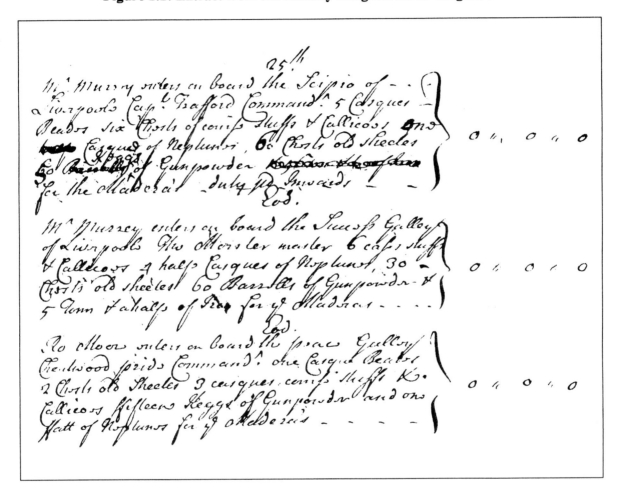

The remainder of the goods were exported on 8 September 1718 by Robert Armitage on the *Owners Adventure*. The master is not named but it was possibly Armitage himself, as he had also loaded goods on the vessel at Liverpool - copper manufactures, pewter, wrought iron and tobacco pipes – for Madeira.[15] Armitage continued in the Guinea trade and between 1730 and 1755 he took part in over fifty voyages, on two occasions as captain.[16]

The Isle of Man's involvement in the Guinea trade had begun (see Appendix 2.2).

2

The Guinea Merchants

Table 2.1: The Top 20 Merchants importing Guinea Goods into the Isle of Man 1718-1764

1	Paul Bridson		11	Mary Reeves
2	William Teare		12	Philip Moore
3	William Murray senior		13	Hugh Cosnahan
4	William Quayle		14	Andrew Savage
5	John Joseph Bacon		15	Ross, Black & Christian
6	Thomas Arthur		16	John Frissel
7	Patrick Savage		17	Edward Moore
8	John Murray		18	Catherine Halsall
9	Robert Kennedy		19	James Oates
10	Phil Finch		20	John Taubman

John Murray was in partnership with his cousin, William Murray senior. William Teare was William Murray's 'confidential clerk' before he became a merchant in his own right. These three men span the period during which the Isle of Man was able to supply the Guinea trade with goods: John Murray died in 1741, William Murray in 1756 and William Teare in 1764. Between them, they imported 15% of the value of Guinea goods that have been identified in the Manx customs records.

This period can be divided into three sections:

Between 1718 and 1723 John Murray and Robert Moore were the main importers of Guinea goods. Moore's involvement in the Guinea trade was short-lived – he died in 1724. There is then a gap in the customs records.

From 1728 to 1745 several Irish merchants had established themselves on the Island – the Reeves family, the Savages and Thomas Arthur. This is when most of the one-off cargoes were imported and the Isle of Man became established within the Guinea trade.

After 1745 the major Manx merchants emerged: Paul Bridson, William Teare, William Quayle and John Joseph Bacon.

John Murray and William Teare had strong connections with two Liverpool merchant houses, the Tarletons and the Davenports, respectively. Although this chapter, and most of the book, tends to concentrate on the Manx links with the Liverpool slave trade, it should be remembered that there were also connections between the Island and the north-west ports of Whitehaven and Lancaster and the Irish and south-west Scottish ports. The emphasis on Liverpool is not merely because it became the leading British slave port but also because to date more information is available about it.

John Murray & Co

One of the earliest Guinea voyages from Liverpool was that of the *Blessing*, which sailed for Africa in 1700. The owners were Thomas Johnson and Richard Norris.[17] Thomas Brownbell was the captain and John Murray the supercargo or 'person charged with the accounts and disposal of the cargo, and all other commercial affairs in the merchant-ship in which he sails'.[18]

The letter of instruction for the voyage was addressed to both Brownbell and Murray. They were to call at Kingsale in Ireland for provisions and then sail with the first fair wind to the Guinea coast. There they were given several alternatives: if there was 'no encouragement' at the Gold Coast they were to sail to Whydah and then Angola where their doctor was 'well-acquainted' and would 'inform you what goods [are] most proper for that place' for the purchase of the slaves. They were exhorted to 'read over your invoice frequently that you may be better acquainted with the goods'. This was because 'the concern we entrust you with is very considerable and will require all your care and diligence to manage it to the best advantage'. Finally Brownbell and Murray were encouraged: 'be assured your diligence shall not go unrewarded. We commit you to the care and protection of the Almighty, who we hope will preserve you from all dangers and crown all our endeavours with success and bring you home with safety'.[19]

It is likely that this John Murray was William Murray senior's brother – and John Murray's cousin. When David Murray, William's brother, died in 1709 his will referred to his brother John as a merchant in Liverpool. This link with an early Guinea voyage would certainly explain the family's subsequent involvement in the Guinea trade.

On the Isle of Man John Murray of Douglas acted both as a sole trader and, with William senior, in several partnerships. Between 1718 and 1741 he imported over £15,000 worth of Guinea goods. Not only did this make him an extremely wealthy man – his properties included Ronaldsway, which he had purchased from William Christian - but also he paid considerable amounts of customs duty, over £2,500. In 1745 when the Duke of Atholl wanted to borrow £12,000 on the security of the customs duties, he assumed that there would be enough money available. As Governor Lindsay explained, however, this was now impossible 'for since old John Murray died our merchants, excepting two or three, have hardly stock enough to carry on their business, and I doubt if any one of these few could spare £1,000 out of trade'.[20]

One of the Murray partnerships was with John Sanforth, described as 'of Douglas' in 1729 but subsequently a Liverpool merchant. Sanforth kept the general accounts of the partnership but the subtle division between the two Murrays was settled privately. After John died, William senior claimed £1,210 was still owed to him. This was paid by the executors without dispute so that there is no a copy of the final account, dated 11 July 1740, in the probate papers. Sanforth was co-owner of one Guinea vessel, the *Lyme*, which sailed from Liverpool on five voyages between 1755 and 1760.[16] She was possibly one of the vessels noted by John Tarleton as expecting to collect gunpowder from the Island in 1759 (see Appendix 2.3a).

A second partnership was between the Murrays, another cousin, John Kelly of Peel, and his brother-in-law, James Gell, also of Peel. This partnership in particular, with all its complexities, makes it extremely difficult to assess the respective rolls played by the individual Manx merchants in the slave trade. James Gell appears to have been the main importer of goods for the smuggling trade - he therefore 'hides' the presence of the Murrays and Kelly in these activities. Gell was an importer of Guinea goods in his own right – although he does not appear in Table 2.1 because he was 32nd on the list. It is not possible to tell whether or not these importations were connected with the Murrays' Guinea trade.

The Tarletons
John Murray probably imported Guinea goods both as a merchant in his own right and as an agent for Liverpool merchants. On 13 August 1719 'Mr Murray for Mr Tarleton & Co' landed from the *Lisle*, Moses Dring master [presumably from Rotterdam], £400 value of goods 'for the Guinea trade' including beads, calico, muslin, silk and copper bars. This complete cargo was collected at Ramsey by Captain John Seacome on board the *Stannage*, himself captain, for Madeira (see Appendix 2.1). She already had on board 17 casks, 2 boxes and 8 chests containing pewter, wrought iron, brass and copper manufactures, looking glasses and British linen and felt hats loaded at Liverpool by Thomas Tarleton.[21] Another Thomas Tarleton vessel, the *Tarleton*, John Tarleton captain, left Liverpool at the same time but it is not known if she also called at the Island on her way to Madeira.[21]

Figure 2.1: Liverpool and the Mersey River

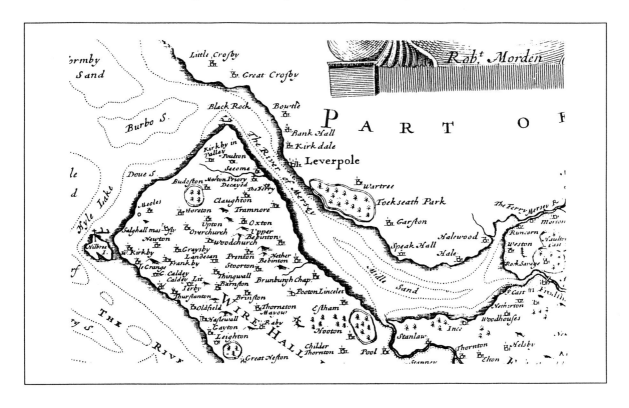

Richardson, in his guide to the Tarleton papers, describes the sequence of generations of John Tarletons as John I, John II etc. It is believed that this was John Tarleton III (1690-1721).[5] Three other Tarletons imported Guinea goods into the Island as follows:

Importer	Date	Vessel	Master	Value
Thomas Tarleton	14 July 1738	*Elizabeth*	Thomas Wingfield	£4,035 16s 8d
Thomas Tarleton	28 February 1739	*Success*	Luke Black	£1,976 0s 0d
John Tarleton	13 June 1739	*Elizabeth*	himself master	£3,024 15s 0d
John Tarleton	4 January 1740	*Frederick*	John Walmsley	£2,536 6s 8d
Isaac Tarleton	5 April 1742	*Neptune*	himself master	£1,029 5s 0d
			Total	£10,602 3s 4d

According to Richardson, Thomas I et al 'fitted out several ventures for Africa' in the 1720s. Both he and his brother, John III, commanded Guinea vessels themselves – in 1721 Thomas was captain of the *Stannage*, when she appears to have called at Cork for further supplies, and John was captain of the *Tarleton*.[22] 'However, with the premature deaths of both Thomas and John, the family's trading activities declined temporarily during the 1730s and early 1740s'.[5] The John and Thomas Tarleton in the Manx records post-date these namesakes.

Both Thomas and Isaac reappear in the customs entries bringing tobacco from Holland on the *Nancy & Sarah* in 1741 and the *North Pole* in 1745, respectively. When Captain Thomas Tarleton died in 1757 he was described as 'of Liverpool now of Douglas'. His only daughter, Jane, was left £10. John Tarleton IV (1718-1773) recorded in his accounts for 1760 that he was owed £12 17s 6d by Gilbert Tarleton.[23] Gilbert was master of John Tarleton's vessel the *Fanny*, which brought brown sugar from Montserrat to the Island in 1761 (see Appendix 2.4c).

The Duke of Atholl used John Tarleton IV as his banker in Liverpool. Revenues collected on the Island would be transported to Liverpool by Charles Lace, master of the *Success* and 'a very careful and very honest man'. Tarleton would acknowledge to the Duke receipt of the money and then it would be remitted by him 'to whom your Grace shall please to order me'.[24] As a result Tarleton had an intimate knowledge of the Duke's income and so he was able to estimate how much of this came by way of customs duties – see Chapter 3.

Other Large Importations
The Tarletons were not the only importers of sizeable single cargoes into the Island. Between 1738 and 1749 there were 70 individual importations of large quantities of India goods: 'one parcel in several cases and trunks'. These are easily distinguishable from the other customs entries as they did not include any details of the contents. They were imported on vessels sailing from a wide range of ports: Rotterdam, Amsterdam, Nantz, Campvere, Bordeaux, Hamburgh and Liverpool. The largest importation was valued at £7,346 and the smallest at £603. The total value was nearly £155,000. The duty was charged at 6d in the pound despite the fact that clearly most, if not all, of these importers were 'strangers', who would normally have paid the higher rate.

In the majority of cases the importations were one-offs. The exceptions are those by John Frampton, Thomas Milner, Pat Stapleton, Pat Starnton and Isaacar Williamson, all of whom were involved in three or more of the importations. Pat Stapleton 'and others' and Pat Starnton made four importations valued at £15,219 and £12,129, respectively.

Some of the customs entries were made by either the master or a supercargo:

Date	Importer	Vessel	Master	Value
1 March 1738	Thomas Alexander	*Neptune*	himself	£3,464 11s 8d
17 February 1742	Abel Anderson	*Notre Dame*	William Anderson	£1,887 3s 4d
16 July 1744	Peter Arthura	*St Michell*	himself	£2,155 16s 8d
3 October 1746	Palmers Ary	*Mermaid*	himself	£2,000 0s 0d

The relationship between Abel and William Anderson is not known. A 'Mr Abel' together with Pat Singleton, imported goods worth £3,404 3s 4d on the *Companions*, Michell Corney master, in January 1741 but there is probably no connection between them.

Each of the large importations was clearly in preparation for the arrival of a particular Guinea vessel at the Island.

Value of Goods	No. of importations
up to £999	11
£1,000 to £2,999	43
£3,000 to £4,999	14
£5,000 plus	2

Presumably these values relate to the sizes of the vessels taking the goods to west Africa. During the same period Guinea goods from smaller importations and valued at over £85,000 were also available on the Island. 395 Guinea vessels sailed from Liverpool and another five from Lancaster between 1738 and 1749.[25] The goods known to have been imported into the Island would probably be sufficient to supply at least half of these vessels. This confirms the suggestion that by the mid 1740s the Isle of Man was playing a significant role in the Guinea trade.

William Murray senior
Between 1731 and his death in 1756 William Murray's importations for the Guinea trade totalled more than £29,000. He was also deeply involved in the smuggling trade and ran a farm and malthouse.

He has not been linked directly with any Liverpool Guinea merchants, although both John Atherton and John Welch made claims against his estate – of £30 and £8, respectively. His kinsman, John Hincks of Chester, acted as 'banker and agent abroad' for Murray. 'His capital in trade being not very considerable he frequently … [was] obliged (when he ordered any merchandise from abroad) to ask for credit'. According to Hincks's current account, dated 21 May 1755, Murray owed £1,250, which he was not in a position to pay at that time. Hincks put a claim into the executor for £1,200.

By the time the partnership with John Murray was dissolved in 1737, William had become blind and infirm and his business affairs were 'long unsettled'. He now married Elizabeth Christian, a widow 'allied to a good family in this Isle and entitled to several houses, concerns and effects in the town of Douglas'. The idea was that she would take charge of his trade books and, by their marriage settlement, was to have £15 a year and 'no share of his fortune'. Elizabeth ran a large dairy, keeping the proceeds in her own hands, and, as Murray complained to William Teare, she must have hoarded up a considerable sum of money during their marriage. Concerned about his own business affairs, Murray instructed his clerk, Henry Allan, to draw up a list of the debts and credits. 'Finding thereby that his affairs were in the utmost confusion, his books lying open and unsettled and several large sums of money due him from persons in desperate circumstances' on 12 July 1756 Murray made a new will. He now gave Elizabeth a legacy of 20 guineas and augmented her annuity to £25. He also left her what parts of his house, garden, household furniture and plate as would be agreed upon between her and his executor.[26] Murray wanted to leave his affairs in 'the hands of a person whom I can depend and rely on seeing them concluded and accomplished'. As a result 'from his known integrity and faithful discharge of whatever he undertakes' he named William Teare as executor.

William Teare
Teare was a considerable merchant in his own right. Between 1746 and 1764 he imported goods worth more than £38,300 so making him the second Guinea importer on the Island, after Paul Bridson (see Table 2.1). Had he not been distracted by the problems of William Murray's estate he might well have outstripped Bridson.

Between William Murray's death and his own death in 1764 Teare was constantly called on to appear in the courts, both on the Island and at York, first to prove that Murray's will had not been forged and that he was the true executor and then to disentangle the debts owed and owing.

Teare left each of his children: William, John, Robert, Edward, Thomas and George the sum of £20. A further £50 was to be 'laid out to pious and charitable uses' at the discretion of his executrix, his wife Charlotte. Finally Charlotte was to 'support and maintain my mother Mrs Catherine Teare during her life in such manner as she has been in during my lifetime'.

The Davenports
There is evidence of Teare's links with Liverpool in the William Davenport letters (see Appendix 2.5). On 26 July 1753 Samuel Sacheverell, captain of the *Charming Nancy*, was instructed to proceed to 'the Isleman' where he was to contact William Teare 'for your Holland cargo, brandy and what other necessaries we have ordered for you'.[27] It has been suggested that this 'Holland cargo' as referring to 'Hollands', which was another name for geneva or gin.[28] A more likely explanation in this context is that the 'Holland cargo' was in fact Guinea goods that had been imported into the Island from Holland. 'Hollands' was also a type of material for the Guinea trade.

The owners of the *Charming Nancy* expected that she would meet with 'all possible dispatch' at Douglas. She was then to 'proceed directly for the river Gambia'. It was not until 28 August, however, that Teare imported on the *Betty*, Stephen Lyds master, from Rotterdam beads, brass pans, cowries and spread eagle dollars valued at £548 10s 3½d together with over 6 tons of iron and 120 doz knives. A delay in the *Charming Nancy*'s voyage is confirmed by the fact that she did not actually sail from Douglas until 8 September 1753.[29] She returned to Liverpool in July 1754.

The *Charming Nancy* was sent to William Teare again, according to her letter of instruction dated 20 August 1754.[30] This time she was accompanied by another Davenport vessel, the *James* with Isaac Hyde master, which was to act as a tender to the *Charming Nancy*. At this stage Teare had beads, textiles and stockfish worth £950 which had been imported on the *Fortune*, Robert Lloyd master, and the *Dorothy*, William Moyser, both from Rotterdam and the *Nancy*, Jacob Caddy, from Cognac.

When the *Charming Nancy* sailed from Liverpool in November 1755, Thomas Dickson was captain. No copy of his letter of instruction has survived but it is known that he collected goods at Douglas before 'in great distress, being tossed about with contrary winds' he was forced into Peel bay. There he contacted George Moore for some 'mere necessaries'. These were supplied 'though he was a stranger to me, having never before seen him'. What aggravated Moore was that he did not receive instant cash. He asked his contact in Liverpool, Robert Kennish, to sort out the payment 'as you would for yourself ... I grudge that it is so delayed'.[31]

The *Charming Nancy* probably encountered further storms in the Irish Sea because Dickson put into Cork for repairs. But before unloading any of the cargo he wrote to his owners. Their reply, dated 23 March 1756, is full of concern that the vessel would be seized if either Dickson or any of the crew, who had been discharged in Ireland, told the authorities that 'you've any India goods on board or that you came from the Isleman'. This was because of an Act aimed at protecting the East India Company and which stated that all goods 'the manufacture or produce of the East Indies' imported into Guernsey, Jersey, Alderney, Sark or Man would be forfeited together with the ship and its 'tackle and furniture'.[32]

14

Dickson had suggested that permission should be obtained from the Irish Customs to discharge his cargo at Cork. 'You do not apprehend [understand] by such an application to them that they would immediately order you to be seized, both ship and cargo. If upon survey you find your vessel worthy of proceeding on your intended voyage, [we] would have you immediately give her the necessary repairs and proceed accordingly, provided you think your cargo is not much damaged. But on the contrary, if you find the vessel unworthy and your cargo rendered unsaleable, we desire you'll patch her up as well as possible to convey your cargo to the Isleman, where our further orders will be lodged for you ... As there is fine weather we hope you may accomplish our orders one way or the other'.

A postscript to the Davenport letter was written by Lawrence Spencer only: 'If you repair the vessel in Ireland and must take out any of the cargo to do it, we desire you'll meddle with neither the Holland goods nor gunpowder. Only the goods shipped here, which you may put in any sloop or covered lighter'.[33]

The *Charming Nancy* did return to the Island because on 3 May 1756 Hugh Cosnahan received one cask containing 4 hundredweight of gunpowder, which had been on board the vessel. There is no evidence of any more of the cargo being relanded, nor is there information about what happened to the vessel: the *Charming Nancy*'s Mediterranean Pass for this voyage was returned on 1 June 1758. This was Dickson's last voyage for the Davenports.

Appendix 2.5 lists other vessels instructed to call at the 'Isleman' for part of their cargoes. Five of these were Davenport vessels. The instructions from William Boats & Co to Ambrose Lace, captain of the *Marquis of Granby*, state: 'With the first favourable wind you must sail and proceed in company with the *Douglas*, Captain Finch, who has some business at the Isle of Man, where you must accompany him, not waiting for him longer than six days'.[34] There is no evidence about the merchant who was to supply Michael Finch, although his brother Phil was in the Guinea trade at this stage. However, there is proof that the *Douglas* called at the Island because according to the customs records John Farran entered 5 hundred and a half of cheese from the vessel.

According to his letter of instruction dated 22 May 1751, William Earle, captain of the *Chesterfield*, was to call at Douglas, Isleman where he was to contact Paul Bridson and take on board 'sundry goods as per list enclosed'.[35] Sadly the list has not survived.

3

The Port of Douglas

Paul Bridson

From 1730 onwards Paul Bridson (see Figure 3.1) appeared regularly in the customs entries for Derbyhaven, importing wool, hides, leather and calf skins from Ireland. Having moved to Douglas, between 1745 and 1764 he imported Guinea goods valued at over £80,000, so becoming the leading merchant on the Island (see Table 2.1). Figure 3.2 shows a sample of the Guinea goods in his customs entries for one day, 20 February 1760.

Bridson was in the anomalous position of being the deputy searcher or customs officer for Douglas while he was also both a merchant in his own right and an agent for others in the Guinea and smuggling trades.

The details of how one merchant received a trunk of East India goods gives an insight into the system. On 26 September 1760 the *Resolution* packet, Peter Blackaller master, arrived at Douglas. [In the customs entries the master is named as Jasper Prendergrass, who also commanded the *Resolution* on some of her voyages – see Table 3.1]. According to letters from Liverpool, a trunk of India goods valued at £241 and two small bags of hops were on board addressed to Thomas Stowell, on behalf of John Stowell & Co. Edward Moore also had a trunk of India goods on board and the merchants went to Castletown together 'to have the same entered' by the comptroller, John Quayle, in the official Customs Ingates and Outgates book (see Figures 1.1, 1.2 and 4.1). They were then given dockets, stating the value of the goods so that the entry fee could be paid (see Figure 3.2). When they returned to Douglas, Moore told Stowell that he would arrange for both lots of goods to be 'turned overboard' that evening by the packet's crew. Stowell 'put up his horse' and went to Bridson's house to pay the entry fee for the India goods and hops. Bridson was not there so Stowell gave the docket and 'the accustomed fee' to his son William, who was 'his deputy'. Stowell walked to the quay where he saw his trunk of India goods in the slings 'waiting his coming to take the same to his house'. Stowell went home 'along with the porters carrying the India goods'. Once there he opened and examined the contents of the trunk and then ordered two of the porters back to the vessel 'to see if the hops were come at and to bring the same home if found'.[36]

As deputy searcher, Bridson or his assistant [son William] was supposed to pay the duty money at Castletown, nine miles away. According to the Commissioners Report of 1792, he had no direct supervisor so that he 'might pay over ... as much or as little as he pleased'. If he were detected then the only punishment would be the loss of a salary of £3 Manx per year. The Duke of Atholl was convinced that 'almost every species of goods and spirits were smuggled in quantities from the duties payable to my family; and that India goods especially were considered as fair game.'[37] It was suspected that Bridson and Quayle divided the resultant profits between them. 'As a corroborating proof of this Bridson died worth a fortune supposed to the amount of £20,000, and Quayle who is still alive, after bringing up a numerous family in a genteel way is supposed to be worth near a third more'.[38] This accusation suggests that any attempt to calculate the total value of Guinea goods imported into the Island must be an underestimate. The records clearly did not include all the goods entered.

Figure 3.2: Extract from the Douglas Ingates 20th February 1760: Paul Bridson's Entries

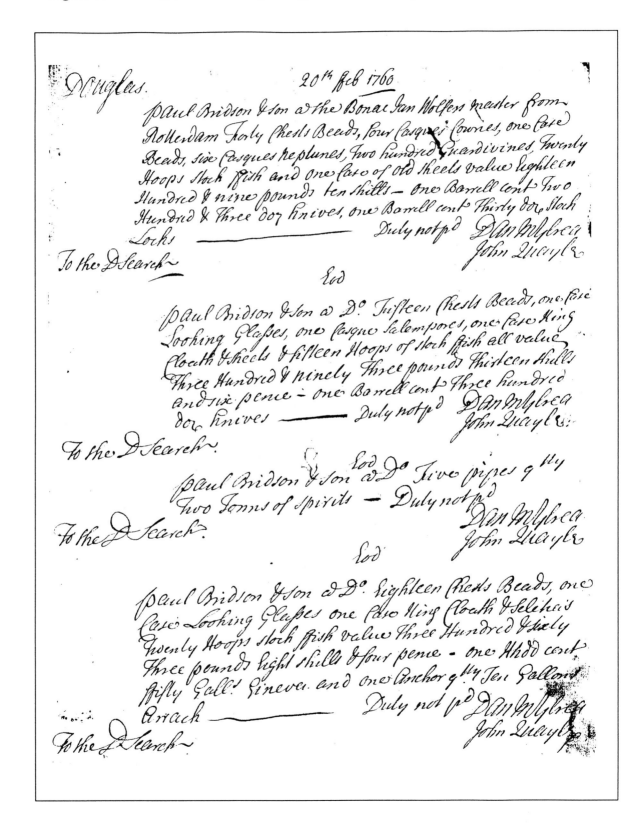

Edward Moore was a major importer of Guinea goods (see Table 2.1) but John Stowell & Co only imported £1,035 worth. Stowell's description of examining the contents of the trunk suggests that these cloths might not have been intended for the Guinea trade. Barcelona handkerchiefs were brought into the Isle of Man in large quantities to be smuggled on to the Irish Sea coasts. It is possible that there was also a market for the Indian handkerchiefs and other cloths. These do appear in small quantities in the inventories produced as part of a will probate. For example, in 1741 Peter Moore of Douglas had in his possession 34 handkerchiefs shalbafts valued at 18s 4½d. Catherine Callister, who died in 1746, had 51 pieces of cotton romals at 10s a piece. Finally in 1762 Daniel Stephenson's shop contained amongst other items 51 single handkerchiefs (best bandanoes) valued at 3s each, 30 chocalee handkerchiefs at 1s 6d each, 15 sooseys at 1s each, 2 whole pieces of calico at 10s per piece, 6 pieces and 7 handkerchiefs [cotton romals] at 10s 6d each, 14 ½ dozen of the best sort of outlandish handkerchiefs at 18s a dozen, 6 dozen of an indifferent sort at 15s, 6 dozen of a bad sort and 7 single ones at 4s and 4½ dozen silk romals at £1 8s per dozen. These goods were auctioned. Jacob Abraham purchased the bandanoes and sooseys and Edward Moore the chocalees.

It is not suggested that these represented more than comparatively small amounts of cloth. Their origin could have been twofold: from the single trunks of East India goods brought in from Liverpool, such as Stowell's trunk described above, or from the 'damnified' or damaged Guinea goods that were returned to the Island (see Chapter 6 and Appendix 2.6). There is a 'tail' of merchants importing East Indian goods valued at less than £100. Sarah Pikeman may have had a shop in Douglas. She imported one trunk of East India goods valued at £59 on the *Charming Molly*, Thomas Callow master, from Liverpool. Although her husband, Alexander Pikeman, a coastal trade master turned merchant, imported over £1,700 worth of Guinea goods, there is no evidence that the two were connected in trade this way. The Guinea goods which were 'damnified' could have been damaged in several ways – if the vessel were caught in a storm then part of the cargo may have got wet, there could have been spillage from something else stored in the hold, or a fire, or rats might have destroyed the containers and some of their contents. Although the damnified goods were no longer suitable for a Guinea cargo some of the individual items could have been in a fit state to sell.

The will inventories also provide evidence of another trend – imitating the East India goods. In the Callister inventory there are 8 yards of Irish persians [tafettas]. In 1750 Mrs Thomas Arthur landed at Douglas 50 dozen culgee handkerchiefs valued at £85 and brought from Rush near Dublin on the *Mary* smuggling wherry, Christopher Farran master. These may have been of Irish manufacture.

Vessels in Douglas: 1760

John Black of Belfast, father of Robert Black one of the partners in Ross, Black & Christian of Douglas, visited the Island in September 1760. He wrote a description of the port in his notebook: 'This Douglas contains about 2,500 inhabitants where refugees for debt from all quarters go. The natives are a superstitious kind of Islanders, with Jews, gentiles, infidels etc etc. At chapel a decent congregation of about 250 persons, the Reverend Moore their pastor. The bay and harbour often thronged with shipping: English colliers, Guinea Liverpoolians, Dutch or other neutrals, about 50 to 60 sail. The town daily increasing in buildings etc'.[39]

Table 3.1 lists the vessels which have been identified from the customs records as being at Douglas on 18 September and 7 October 1760. This suggests that Black was not exaggerating the amount of shipping. A list of eight possible Guinea 'Liverpoolians', which had sailed from their home port between 1 September and 3 October 1760 is included in Appendix 2.7. The *Dove* and the *Young James*, were reported as being at the Island in 1761 (Appendix 2.8).[16]

Table 3.1: 'The Bay and Harbour often thronged with Shipping':

**Home Ports of Vessels mentioned in the Customs Entries for Douglas
on 18 September and 7 October 1760**

Barry: the *Little Betty*, Isaac Nicholas;
Carnarvon: the *Golden Apple*, William Williams and *Hopewell*, John Williams;
Chester: the *Tryall*, Owen Evans;
Cork: the *Bonetta*, Henry Lee;
Dublin: the *Lark*, Lawrence Crosthwait and *Patrick*, John Crenane;
Dutton: the *Betty & Mary*, William Atkinson;
Ellenfoot (later known as Maryport): the *Happy Return*, Daniel Allen and *Parr*, John Williams;
Lancaster: the *James*, John Rimer;
Liverpool: the *Eagle*, Thomas Williams, *Hope*, John Hall, *Lamb*, Robert Kelly, *Lark*, Rice Evans, *Molly*, George Torford, *Molly*, Joseph Tordiff, *Morning Star*, Thomas Folks, *Sarah*, Joseph Dressor, *Success*, David Evans, *Success*, Richard Rose and the *Resolution*, Jasper Prendergrass
Newport: the *Leight*, John Duns and *Maria*, John Nicholas;
Preston: the *Clater*, John Taterson and *Peggy*, Thomas Ashton;
Rostraver and Newry: the *James*, James Morton;
Rush: the *Patrick*, Patrick Caine, *Patrick*, Michael Connor, and *Patrick*, Thomas Knight;
Swansea: the *John and Martha*, - Lewhellin;
Wales (port unspecified): the *Charming Betty*, Evan Humphries;
Wexford: the *John*, John Rosen;
Whitehaven: the *Good Intent*, John Barber, *Hope*, John Fall, *Hopewell*, David Davies and *Maxwell*, Jonathan Shelton;
Rotterdam: the *Morgenstar*, William Christian, (see Appendix 3.3)

Black was also impressed by son Robert's house, which he described as an 'elegant dwelling'.[39] There is a considerable amount of information available in the wills of the Guinea trade merchants, and of the slave captains, about the properties which they owned both on the Island and in England. An analysis of the sources of this property has become part of a larger study. In addition to the Guinea trade, it may have come from smuggling, or it may have been acquired quite legitimately from inheritance or marriage settlements.

The Dutch Cargoes
Black mentioned the 'Dutch or other neutrals'. Merchants on the Island had been involved in trade with Rotterdam as a source of 'high duty and prohibited goods' from the early 1700s. It was a simple step to add the items suitable for a Guinea cargo – and to warehouse them on the Island until a vessel called on its way to the African coast. These items would be purchased in Holland from the Dutch East India Company by agents acting either for the Manx or the Liverpool merchants [or merchants from other slaving ports] and transported from Rotterdam usually on Dutch vessels with Dutch masters.

Between 1718 and 1764 over 190 such voyages were made by more than 100 masters who brought to the Island Guinea goods valued at nearly £224,000. Jan Wolfers, master of first the *Vrede* and then the *Marquis de Bonac*, undertook at least 44 of these voyages and was responsible for 28% of the total imports. An analysis of the goods which he delivered to the Island is given in Appendix 3.4.

20

The main merchants importing goods on the Jan Wolfers vessels were:

Paul Bridson	41% total value
William Teare	12%
William Quayle	10%

Michael Somers replaced Wolfers as master of the *Vrede* [*Peace*] between 1755 and 1761. He made a further eleven voyages in the vessel.

The Thomas Mears Vessels

East Indian goods were imported into the Island in contravention of an Act 'of which the main objective was to secure and extend the monopoly of the East India Company'.[32] In Chapter 2 reference was made to Davenport & Co's concern in case Thomas Dickson unloaded some of the *Charming Nancy*'s cargo at Cork. Vessels that had taken the East Indian goods to the Island were also at risk of being seized. This Act was originally passed in 1720. Yet there appeared to be few attempts to seize the Dutch vessels on their voyages to or from the Island. Eventually new trading networks developed and the vessels began to call regularly at Liverpool. There was great indignation amongst the Liverpool merchants when suddenly seizures were made.

In 1763 Paul Bridson, together with William Quayle and other Manx merchants, had imported at Douglas Guinea goods from three Dutch vessels (see Appendix 3.5 for details of the *Henrietta Maria*'s cargo). On leaving the Island, all these vessels were due to call at Liverpool, where their contact was Thomas Mears. When they arrived there, they were seized by Arthur Onslow, a king's customs officer.

Vessel & master	Date seized	Reason for seizure
Henrietta Maria, Hendrick Bremer	5 May 1763	Importing 8 casks French brandy pretending it to be Rhenish. Even after a certificate had been produced from Holland, counter-signed by the British Consul there, proving that the brandy did not from France, the vessel was still detained
Marquis de Bonac Jan Wolfers	16 June 1763	'Illegal landing of teas' – location not specified
John Hans Neilson	12 July 1763	Because of the goods she had landed at the Isle of Man

Mears had to instruct his correspondent in London to pay £2,690 into the Court of Exchequer, as security, before the ships were allowed to return to Rotterdam. He then reported the problem to the Duke of Atholl. Onslow's seizures would in future 'restrain foreigners from carrying on a trade to the Island which they have so long enjoyed unmolested'. The financial implications of the vessels having been seized were so great that 'no sensible man' would attempt landing goods on the Island in future and 'under these circumstances the African trade must suffer and the revenues of the Island decline'. Some of the Liverpool merchants had proposed to call a meeting but nothing had been arranged as yet. However, they did feel 'intimidated and every branch of business interested in that valuable commerce is suffering therefore if you can point out any steps necessary to be taken it will oblige many of the African traders here'.[40]

Christopher Hasell, also a merchant in Liverpool, confirmed that the *Henrietta Maria* had been seized because of the French brandy on board. As he wrote to his brother Ned at Rotterdam 'how it will end I can't tell'. Ned had sent two half pounds of tea, one of singlo and the other souchong to Liverpool on the *Bonac*. These were to be delivered to 'our good mother at Dalemain, being a sample of Dutch tea'.[41] The correspondence between the Hasell brothers also referred to cargoes of pimento being sent from Liverpool on the *Bonac* to Rotterdam. This effectively completes the *Bonac*'s voyage: Guinea and East Indian goods from Rotterdam to the Isle of Man, some additional items from the Island to Liverpool and goods that had been imported into Liverpool, possibly by way of the Guinea trade, back to Rotterdam. It also emphasises the large number of merchants with an interest in any particular voyage.

The Liverpool Trunks
Several trunks of East India goods were imported directly from Liverpool. On 26 February 1751 Hugh Cosnahan landed from the *Success*, Charles Lace master, six trunks and one box of India goods valued at £1,007 3s 10d. Details of their contents are given in Appendix 3.6.

Goods worth nearly £152,500 were imported in this way on some 370 voyages. The masters of the vessels were either Manx or from Liverpool. Oliver Garner, who was responsible for over 50 of the voyages, appears to have come from Liverpool. Henry Woods [43 voyages], John Moore [34], Charles Lace [32] and Nicholas Shimmin [27] all came from the Island.

It is not clear why so many trunks of East India goods came from Liverpool to be loaded on a Guinea vessel, which had to call at the Island specifically for them. One possibility is that the duties already paid at Liverpool could be 'drawn back' or repaid on exportation of the goods sooner rather than later. They would then pay the lower Island duty. Also it gave the merchant or the captain of the vessel a chance to 'sort' the cargo before it actually arrived on the African coast (see the response from the Board of Customs on page 1).

Guinea vessels calling at the Isle of Man
At first the presence of the Guinea vessels at the Island was recorded in the Customs Outgates (see Figure 1.2). No duty was payable on goods exported which had already paid duty on importation and by the early 1720s the Liverpool vessels are no longer mentioned. Details of Guinea goods exported do appear from time to time, however, in the Outgates (see Chapter 4). By the time the Dukes of Atholl became Lords of the Isle, the system had changed. The only Outgates recorded were those where duty was payable. For example, there were 'Nil' Outgates recorded in 1741 while the total export duty in 1752 was 4s 10d, all for limestones.

It is clear from other sources, however, that the Guinea vessels did continue to call at the Island (see Appendix 2). They fall into two categories: <u>certain</u> like those reported as calling at the Isle of Man or wrecked there and <u>possible</u> like the Guinea vessels that may have been seen by John Black and the six gunpowder vessels noted by John Tarleton (see below).

<u>Gunpowder</u>
As the agent of a London gunpowder manufacturing company, Christopher Hasell was constantly aware of any competition, particularly from powder available on the Isle of Man (see Chapter 6). He suspected Miles Barber, another Liverpool merchant, of lodging Dutch powder there. In fact on 23 January 1753 Phil Finch imported 10 barrels of gunpowder weighing 10 hundred weight on the *Concord*, Walter Barber master, from Rotterdam.

On 13 April 1759 Colin Campbell, commander of the *Prince George* revenue cruiser, seized the *Isabel* brig, Walter Dougal [or Dugdale] master. This was a Scottish vessel sailing from Rotterdam to the Isle of Man with 600 barrels of ordinary gunpowder, a quantity of spirits and a small parcel of muskets, 'suitable only for the Guinea trade'. Campbell took the vessel first to Campbeltown and then into the Clyde.

According to John Tarleton, six Liverpool Guinea ships were expecting to collect the *Isabel*'s gunpowder at Douglas (see Appendix 2.3a). These included the *Blackburne*, which was a Tarleton vessel, the *Lyme*, which was co-owned by John Sanforth and Thomas Mears and the *Isaac*, David Clatworthy master, which was a Richard Townsend & Co vessel[16] – see below. As Tarleton explained to the Duke of Atholl, the powder had been ordered from the Island because 'our stills are stopped in England and gunpowder is scarcely to be had at any price'. He did not think that obtaining gunpowder by this method was against the law. However, he forewarned that 'if we are debarred this recourse we may give up the trade'.

Tarleton hoped that the Duke of Atholl would use his influence at London 'to have this ship immediately discharged and that for the future the trade may not be interrupted by such illegal seizures'.[42] The Duke replied on 4 May 1759: 'I should be very glad to be of any service upon this occasion but I am afraid it would be looked upon as too delicate a point for me to interfere in. Besides I am at a loss to know to whom and in what manner to make any application. If you can be of any hint concerning this I shall let you know how far it may be fitting for me to interpose'.

Fortunately the vessel was released in early July, as George Baird of Glasgow reported to the Duke.[43] On 30 July 1759 Paul Bridson landed from the *Isabel* 570 barrels of gunpowder weighing 50,000 lbs, 1 cask and 44 bags of gun flints, 17 chests of guns and 5 boxes of pistols together with geneva, arangoes, knives, ling fish, looking glasses, silesias, spirits and stockfish. There is no information about what happened to the other 30 barrels of gunpowder.

Tarleton also noted that 'Your Grace's revenue in the Isle of Man has been greatly increased by the many cargoes we have landed there from Holland for our Guinea ships'. As already noted, Tarleton was the Duke's banker in Liverpool and so he was in an excellent position to guess how much of the Island's revenue came from the customs duties on imported goods. For example he had received from Charles Lace in November 1757 £800, December 1757 500 guineas, February 1758 £1,353, May 1758 £1,000 and April 1759 £1,500.[44]

An analysis has been made of the Guinea goods component of the customs duties for 1754 – it was only 10.9%, compared with 7.6% for teas [also from the East Indies]. This exercise, however, did not include the rum duties for importations also directly linked with the slave trade – see Chapter 6.

In 1802 the value of the India goods brought from Liverpool between 10 October 1753 and 10 October 1763 was calculated. They accounted for 2% of the total duties. This figure, however, should be disregarded. The ticks still exist in the margins of at least one of the Customs Ingates and Outgates books. From these it can be seen that, for no apparent reason, some of the entries were omitted. This is an excellent example of the potential problems caused by using secondary information.[45]

There was another problem over gunpowder, this time involving Richard Townsend & Co. On 27 December 1758 Bridson, acting as their agent, had landed 18 barrels of gunpowder at Douglas. No evidence has been found of this entry but by that date the Ingates books no longer exist so that it would have been very easy for a loose entry docket to go missing. In April 1759 ten of these barrels had been shipped on board the *Jane*, captain Daniel Hayes, 'bound for the coast of Guinea'. The following May, Bridson was required to detain the remaining 8 barrels in his custody for six months or 'till the further order from his Majesty'.[46] Although another Townsend vessel, the *Isaac*, David Clatworthy captain, sailed from Liverpool in May 1759,[16] there is no further information about what happened to the rest of the gunpowder.

William Boats

Paul Bridson had links with William Earle, Thomas Mears, John Tarleton and Richard Townsend, all Liverpool merchants. But his most significant Liverpool link was with William Boats, who was the second leading British slave merchant between 1785 and 1795.[47] In 1760 he became engaged to Elizabeth Bridson. Their names appear on the probate papers for her brother, Thomas, who died in 1766.

Boats has become a somewhat legendary figure. It is often stated that he was found abandoned in an open boat on the Liverpool dockside, taken to an orphanage and given the surname Boats there. His birth is recorded, however, in the IGI as the son of James Boats, born in 1716. Having started life as 'a beggar', Boats became a slave ship captain. He had a 'swashbuckling career' – when commander of the *Knight*, he had a dispute with the natives at Anamaboe and five years later armed some slaves to help in the fight against a French privateer[16] – see Chapter 8. Having co-owned some of the vessels he mastered, Boats then settled down in Liverpool as a merchant in his own right. On 2 March 1759 George Moore reported to Haliday & Dunbar, Liverpool merchants, that Mr Boats 'who was connected with Mr Knight in trade' had viewed Peel harbour and thought Moore's proposal for its enlargement 'worthy of further consideration'.[48]

Table 3.2: Guinea Vessels owned by William Boats & Co in 1790[49]

Vessel	Tons	Seamen	Vessel & Outfit	Cargo	Total Value
Jane	242	35	£3,907 6s 9d	£7,287 19s 4d	£11,195 6s 1d
Vulture	315	43	£5,699 10s 4d	£8,513 17s 6d	£14, 213 7s 10d
Gregson	258	40	£5,300 0s 0d	£9,700 0s 0d	£15,000 0s 0d
Eliza	348	40	£7,103 17s 7d	£8,766 0s 0d	£15,869 17s 7d
King Peppel	323	40	£6,757 9s 1d	£8,621 6s 6d	£15,378 15s 7d
Ann	222	36	£4,822 19s 5d	£6,992 6s 7d	£11,815 6s 0d
Mary Ann	136	26	£3,521 4s 11d	£5,329 3s 9d	£8,850 8s 8d
Squirrel	180	36	£4,502 17s 5d	£2,600 14s 6d	£7,103 11s 11d
Ranger	110	25	£3,100 0s 0d	£284 10s 0d	£3,384 10s 0d
Thomas	265	35	£5,500 0s 0d	£9,000 0s 0d	£14,500 0s 0d
Betsey	143	30	£4,030 0s 0d	£5,300 0s 0d	£9,330 0s 0d
Totals	2542	386	£54,245 5s 6d		£126,701 3s 8d
			Insurance at	£6 per £100	£8,060 0s 0d
					£134,761 3s 8d

His reputation at Liverpool is confirmed by Hugh Crow: 'My great aim, however, was to get into the very respectable employ of W. Boats, Esq. And to my great satisfaction I was appointed second mate (equal to chief mate in any other employ) of his ship, the *Jane*, Reuben Wright, master, bound to Bonny on the coast of Africa'.[4] This vessel sailed from Liverpool in June 1792. Boats died in 1794, aged 78. His obituary in the Liverpool newspaper noted: 'William Boates's extensive transactions in the commercial world rendered him a most useful member of society and his memory will be long revered by all who had connections with him'.[8]

Elizabeth was already dead. Boats left each of his daughters, Elizabeth and Ellen, £13,000. His partner in trade, Thomas Seaman, was to receive one hundred guineas, all the servants five guineas a piece and the rest of the estate went to his son.[50] Henry Ellis Boats sold the remaining three vessels.[47] He died in January 1805 at Rosehill, Denbighshire.

4

The Irish and Other Connections

Mary Reeves

Several Irish merchants settled on the Isle of Man during the early years of the Guinea trade. These included Robert and Mary Reeves, Patrick and Andrew Savage and Thomas Arthur. Their presence was not welcomed by the native Manx merchants, who valued their rights of priority when debts were to be paid either from the effects of someone who had 'failed' in business or from the estate of someone who had died on the Island, owing money. Considering that there were rarely sufficient sums of money to cover all the debts, this was an extremely valuable right. The natives were also concerned about the religious persuasion of some of these 'strangers'.

When Garret Byrn died intestate, Robert and William Reeves, and Thomas Arthur, claimed that they had an equal right with William Murray senior and Philip Finch in the payment of the debts due. As they were strangers, they lost their case, not only on the Island but also before Lord Mansfield, the commissioner of appeals to the Duke of Atholl in London. This having 'proved fruitless and abortive' in 1757 Francis Dean of Douglas, 'an Irish papist', petitioned the Duke for naturalisation. As Dean was 'well recommended' by the Governor, the Duke agreed that he should have all the privileges of a native, provided he made an oath and paid a 'fine' of £3 17s 9d. The Duke subsequently naturalised three more Irish papists – the Reeves brothers and Thomas Arthur. In 1759 John Callin of Peel, Thomas Moore of Douglas and John Stevenson of Castletown petitioned the Duke asking that these naturalisations should be 'rescinded'. They did not win their cause and more 'strangers' continued to arrive in the Island.[51]

Thomas Arthur imported over £16,900 worth of Guinea goods into the Island, Patrick Savage £14,700 and Andrew Savage £8,800. Francis Dean does not appear to have been involved in this trade.

Many Irish merchants who were present on the Island still had connections back home. Reference has been made already to John Black's visit to his son Robert (see Chapter 3). Part of the reason for this visit was to discuss business. John Black's sister was married to James Arbuckle, at one stage one of the wealthiest of the Belfast merchants.[52] Arbuckle's son, another James, died on the Island in May 1739. He had been on his way to Whitehaven [his father-in-law was Walter Lutwidge – see below] when he was put into Peel by 'contrary winds'. He had been 'very much out of health' for some time and died the following day.[53]

Patrick Stacpole made three importations of Guinea goods worth £828 16s 7d. He is mentioned in a letter from William Murray senior at Douglas to Allen Stanley, the comptroller at Castletown, dated 2 September 1737. This letter refers to the duty Murray owed for India goods. [There is no reference to this importation in the Ingates – nor to one by Stacpole]. Little else is known about Patrick Stacpole. Francis Stacpole, however, was a Cork merchant during this period, competing 'aggressively for a share of the Caribbean market'.[54]

The case of the *Hope* dogger

On 26 June 1750 the *Hope* dogger, John Bordero master, arrived at Douglas from Rotterdam with East India goods on board for Thomas Arthur. This was one of the occasions when the English customs officers did attempt to seize a vessel bringing India goods to the Island. Captain Dow of the *Sincerity* revenue cruiser from Whitehaven was already in Douglas harbour and he sent some of his men on board. The master, realising that they were customs officers, claimed that he was bound for Dronton in Norway. This was a standard ruse used by a vessel when boarded in the wrong place at the wrong time. The reason given was that they were there because of 'stress of weather'. To confirm the captain's story, the *Hope* headed northwards.[55]

In his capacity as deputy searcher at Douglas, Paul Bridson 'ventured on board' the *Sincerity* 'in a civil manner' to serve Captain Dow with a writ to appear next morning 'to show his authority' for acts of violence within a port of the Island – boarding a smuggling wherry from Ireland and attempting to seize a vessel from Rotterdam. 'Instead of being admitted to see Dow, Bridson was ill-used by some of the crew so that the action could not be served without hazard of life. Dow's son treated Bridson contemptuously and threw him down off the quarter-deck, which might have ruined him. But providently he got no hurt'.[56]

Figure 4.1 Extract from the Ramsey Ingates for 12 July 1750

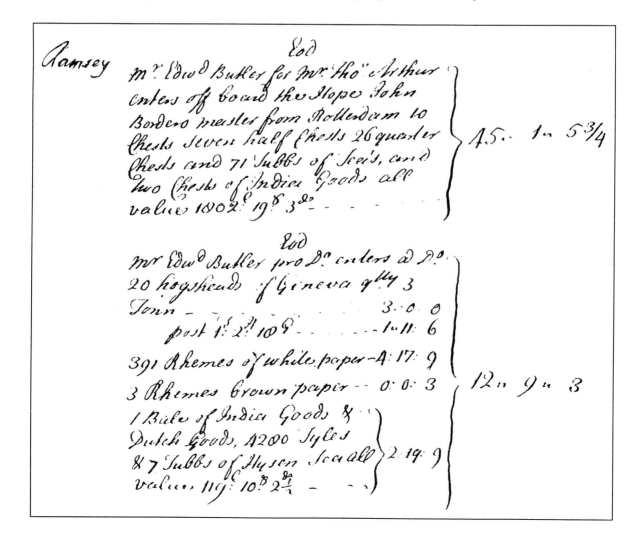

The *Sincerity* followed the *Hope* to Ramsey but once more failed to seize her. The English customs officers tried again. On 28 December 1750 Dow's son and Sidebotham, the king's customs officer on the Island, demanded copies of the entries for the goods landed from the *Hope*. John Quayle replied that the customs book was not a public record but the Duke's private account.[57] Figure 4.1 shows that Edward Butler, as Thomas Arthur's agent, had in fact managed to import an assorted cargo of India goods, tea, geneva, paper and tiles at Ramsey.

The Reeves Family

When Robert Reeves died in 1738 Mary continued to deal 'largely in all kinds of goods'. Between 1742 and her death on 9 March 1747 she imported over £11,000 worth of Guinea goods, which represented 14% of the total during that period. When she died it was said that she had been 'very rich'.[58] However, there were ten children to inherit the fortune. The eldest son, Robert, was an attorney in Dublin with an estate in Ireland of £500 a year, and two daughters were already married – Hester to Thomas Heywood of Nunnery Howe, Douglas. William was currently abroad and the two youngest daughters, Deborah and Amelia, were underage, so that they chose their brother-in-law Heywood, 'who has a good estate' and their brother Robert as their supervisors.

Mary Reeves's last importation of Guinea goods was on 24 February 1747. On 4 June Robert imported goods worth £277, possibly already ordered by his mother. He appears again in 1748 with four separate importations totalling over £1,300. By 1749 William was in partnership with him. The Reeves brothers were not experienced in trade. One of their mistakes was over-diversification – they imported rum from Barbados, geneva and tea from Rotterdam, brandy from Saloe; they purchased Andrew Bermingham's tobacco manufactory; they continued to deal in Guinea goods. At the same time they tended not to pay their debts. In 1755 they still owed John Lewhellin of Ramsey £275 for 100 bandanoes purchased in April 1748 and Hugh Cosnahan £170 18s 5d 'for certain goods and merchandise sold and delivered'. In the meantime they had failed, owing considerable sums of money.

Robert Reeves, who had kept the accounts for the partnership, left the Island. William had to be supported on charity. He went briefly to Dumfries in an attempt to collect some of the debts owing for goods already smuggled into Scotland and to win new orders. Reeves then returned to Douglas where Heywood attempted to support him so that he would be able, in time, to clear his own debts. The support appears to have taken the form of persuading Paul Bridson to give Reeves credit, on Heywood's security. This was only a verbal agreement but it did cement Heywood's position with the 'strangers' at Douglas.

One of George Moore's complaints about the proposal to build a new bridge across the harbour (see next chapter) was that this had divided the merchant community in Douglas. 'The party for the bridge is headed by Mr Heywood, whose lands lying contiguous to the harbour on the south side give room to suspect that his private interest is his motive. The strangers in Douglas join him and as several of these were lately naturalise their being advocates of the bridge gives room to suspect that the governor of our Isle [Basil Cochrane] is for the bridge. The party against the bridge is the native inhabitants'.[59]

On 7 November 1756 the Chancery Court found in Cosnahan's favour – his debt was to be repaid by Reeves. This should have been done by first arresting and then selling all the Reeves property and goods still on the Island. In the meantime, however, Heywood had taken possession of everything, against a debt owed to him of £500. No money was forthcoming. Then on 3 December 1762 the decision of the Manx court was reversed at Lincoln's Inn. This was because Deborah Reeves was also owed a considerable sum of money. Still a spinster,

27

living in Dublin, she described herself as a 'helpless woman'. She had been due £585 17s 3¼d from her mother's estate and, as she trusted Heywood, she left this money in his care. So far she had received a couple of interim payments but was still owed £483 6s 8d. The case dragged on for so long that by 1772, with interest at 5%, it totalled £844 3s 4¾d. By this time Thomas Heywood was dead but his son Peter John Heywood insisted that she should have her money in full.[60] As a result Deborah had 'usurped' the rights of the native Manx, Cosnahan. This was only one of Cosnahan's many financial disappointments during the period after the Revestment Act changed the Island's role so that it was no longer a warehouse for goods.

Figure 4.2 The Isle of Man and the Irish Sea Connections

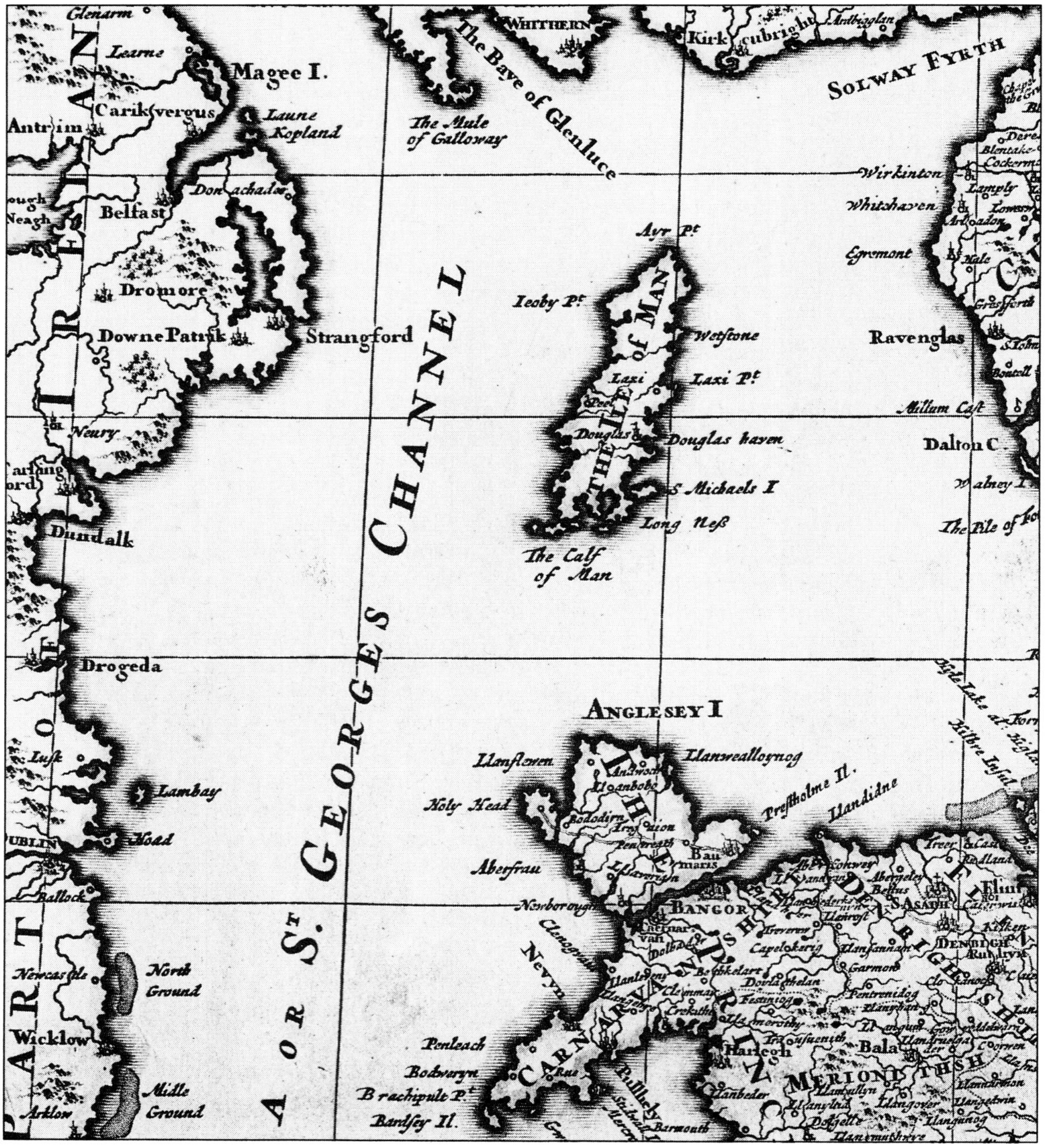

While the Irish merchants on the Island tended to import goods for the English Guinea ships, there is also a suggestion of links between the Island and Ireland and Scotland in the Guinea trade itself.

The Irish Connection

On 18 May 1713 Charles Warean landed from the *Francis* sloop of Dublin, Edward Huggins captain, eight boxes containing 600 piece longees, 'five of which boxes were damnified goods' so that the total value was only £250 [in 1737 a longee romal was valued at 16s per piece – see page 4]. The fact that the boxes were 'damnified' suggests that the *Francis* had received storm damage at some stage in her voyage. There is no information, however, about where she had come from before landing these goods.

In September of that year John Murray of Douglas imported East Indian cloths that had been brought to the Island on the *Ross* of Castletown, John Kewish master, from Dublin. These included 1,120 yards of calico and the total duty paid was £7 15s 9d so that the value of the other cloths must have been about £120. The *Ross* sailed on to Liverpool. Eight months later, in May 1714, Murray put on board the *Francis*, Edward Huggins still captain, a trunk of cloths, which was not liable to duty because it contained 'part of the goods imported here out of the *Ross* of Castletown'.[61] Once more no further information has been found on the Island about where the *Francis* took this trunk of goods.

It has been noted already that the vessels actually heading for Guinea often cleared out 'for the Maderas'. There is also evidence of Guinea cargoes being sent first to Bilbao, Lisbon, Bordeaux and Guernsey (see Appendix 2.11). Daniel Morton exported both tobacco and calico on the *Robert* of Wexford, Pat Carnoy captain, in June 1718 for Bilbao. This was a comparatively small cargo. In 1731, however, Patrick Murphey, captain of the *Margaret*, carried two trunks, three portmanteau and four bales of India goods there. Either the *Margaret* was herself a Guineaman or these goods were to be collected at Bilbao by another vessel en route for west Africa.

Christopher Denn imported 21 boxes and 3 bales of East Indian cloths valued at £1,200 on board the *Liver*, John Lawson master in January 1720. These were all exported in February on the *Betty* of Dublin, Pat Coody, for Lisbon. This suggests a similar situation to that of the *Margaret*.

When boats sailed from a port on the Island with 'prohibited and high duty goods' for England, Ireland, Scotland or Wales, the destination of their voyage was often disguised. According to the entry in the customs book they had gone coastwise to another Island port. As a result the Outgates are a rich source of information about the smuggling trade as they record thousands of gallons of brandy and other goods going coastwise from Douglas to Peel etc, with information about the merchant loading the boat, the boat's name and its master. It is probable that the omission of this detail from the Outgates after 1735 is because it was realised that should the customs books fall into the wrong hands then they would provide excellent ammunition for those wishing to attack the rights of the Duke of Atholl, and of the Island itself.

There are also records in the Outgates of several boats sailing from Douglas to Peel or Port St Mary with various quantities of Guinea goods on board. In 1720 Patrick Savage sent Guinea goods from Peel to Douglas on the *Hopewell*, Edward Hopes a local Manx trader master, and in 1721 to Derry on the *Jane*, Jo Abernethy master. There are numerous other examples but it is unclear at this stage how many of the supposed coastal short hauls were in fact going elsewhere.

Walter Lutwidge

Lutwidge, born in Dublin but based as a merchant at Whitehaven, had several correspondents on the Island, including Thomas Arthur and John Murray of Douglas. His own agent, Richard Goodman, was sent to live at Ramsey. Lutwidge's main trade was in tobacco, wine and brandy. He used the Island regularly to land and reship goods.[52] In 1720 Murray sent wine which had been imported from Spain on the Lutwidge vessel *Queen of Sheba* to Whitehaven on the *Stanhope*, another Lutwidge vessel, and to Sarkfoot on the *Hopewell* of Carlisle.

Figure 4.3: Whitehaven

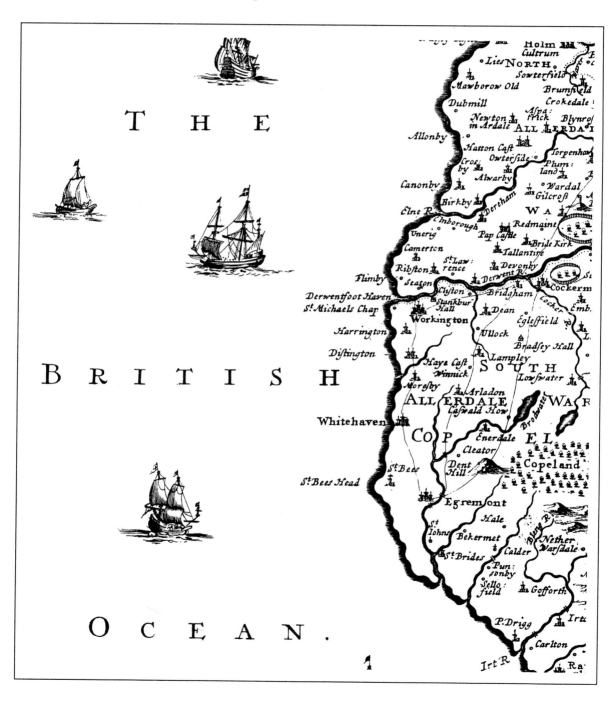

Lutwidge also claimed to have supplied part of the goods for several Guinea voyages and the details of these cargoes are set out in his letter-book.[62] While it is suspected that the goods came from the Island, no direct proof of this has been found to date. Goodman imported comparatively small amounts of Guinea goods during the 1730s – valued at £70. Although some of the items do correspond with the Lutwidge Guinea cargoes, they represent only a small fraction of the total. Goodman later moved to Dublin, where he became a tobacco merchant in his own right. In 1751 he was in partnership with Thomson & Bertrand in the *Dolphin*, Joseph Pedrick captain. This vessel only undertook one Guinea voyage. In 1753 she was lost in a hurricane in the Gulf of Florida on her homeward voyage from Jamaica to Liverpool.[16]

Christopher Denn had links with the Whitehaven Guinea trade. In 1720 he imported on the *Ann* of that port, Thomas Lamb captain, several Indian cloths which were only valued at £60 'being damnified'. He was no longer on the Island in the 1730s and so could not have supplied Lutwidge. At the same time there is no evidence that the Lutwidge voyages sailed from Whitehaven.[63] In 1749 Lutwidge wrote to John Hardman at Liverpool that 'it would not be disagreeable to me to be concerned a little in the Guinea trade from your place as I have ships and no employment for them'. He then emphasises his lack of faith in Whitehaven as a slaving port. Hardman would have to nominate the captain and officers of the vessel 'necessary to be skilled in the trade, people here being strangers to it'.[52]

The Scottish Connection

It is likely that at least one of Lutwidge's Guinea voyages sailed from Kirkcudbright. It is also possible that the captain was William Patten. In a letter dated 1740 Lutwidge claims to have saved Patten from his 'scrapes with relation to the Kirkcudbright [smuggling] company'. He then made him commander of a ship, which he 'sent round the world to transport passengers over to settle his plantation in Virginia'.[52]

In 1743 Thomas Williamson imported at Douglas from on board the *St Dennis*, Charles Groves master, several chests and cases of India goods, teas and chinaware valued at £3019 18s 4d. With Joseph Farmer, John Hardman, William Spencer and John Strong, Williamson was a co-owner of the *King of Sardinia*. She undertook two voyages to Africa in 1746 and 1748 with a Williamson as captain on the first voyage as far as Barbados and then John Maddock captain for the remainder of that voyage and the next. Although Williamson is described as a Liverpool merchant, the vessel was lost at Kirkcudbright on her way from Jamaica to Liverpool in 1750.[16] She had probably gone into the Solway to unload some of her West Indian cargo of rum. In a letter dated 1748 Walter Lutwidge mentions a Williamson in the Kirkcudbright area.

Isaacar Williamson was a major importer of India goods - 'several cases, trunks and boxes' came into Douglas:

Date	Vessel	Master	Value
4 January 1740	*Success*	William Thompson	£2,452
2 August 1740	*Success*	Thomas Conran	£3,342
12 December 1740	*Nancy*	Thomas Milton	£3,473
2 April 1741	*Nancy*	Luke Black	£3,713

He could possibly have been part of the same partnership.

On 21 August 1751 Patrick Mitchell imported at Douglas on the *Methuen*, John Coppell captain, beads, India or Guinea goods, old sheets, gunpowder, brass ware, iron bars, guns and

31

pistols, flints, cutlasses, knives and earthenware from Rotterdam. She then went to Greenock before sailing from Liverpool in October, presumably calling at the Isle of Man again for her cargo before heading for the Guinea coast. Mitchell was one of the owners of the vessel, who were all from Glasgow. The captains were Duncan Campbell from Greenock to Liverpool and then William Cockran and John Somervill on the Guinea voyage.[16]

The following year the *Thistle*, James McCulloch captain, arrived at Ramsey from St Eustatia. She had a cargo of rum on board which was imported by Ross, Black & Christian, David Forbes, Edward Christian and a John Wallace. William Teare also imported a cask of cotton chelloes and a case of nicannees valued at £97 15s 7d, which were probably surplus to requirements. There is no evidence of this vessel in the Liverpool Trade and Shipping database, although she was probably in the Guinea trade. John McCulloch of Kirkcudbright was used by the governor and the Duke of Atholl as a means of sending correspondence to and from the Isle of Man, until Dow of the *Sincerity* revenue cruiser seized the Island's account rolls from the packet boat as she arrived at Kirkcudbright in 1750.[64] After that date the correspondence went by way of Liverpool and McCulloch moved to the Island, where he imported Guinea goods worth £250. His son, James, joined him as a merchant and after Revestment they moved first to Guernsey and then to Dunkirk.

5

Manx Harbours and the Guinea Trade

George M[oore] [signature]

George Moore (Figure 5.1), based at Peel on the west coast of the Isle of Man, was a major merchant of the smuggling trade.[65] His influence on the Island's Guinea trade, however, was more as a local politician than directly as a merchant. Together with his brother Philip, Moore campaigned against the building of a new bridge across Douglas harbour. When this opposition failed, George Moore then turned his attention to the enlargement of Peel harbour, to attract the Guinea vessels there, away from the east coast.

Figure 5.1 George Moore (1709 - 1787)

Moore did not import large numbers of Guinea goods – total value less than £1,000. One reason for this could be that, as he knew only too well, Peel was rarely used by the Guinea vessels, which tended to favour Douglas. Another possibility is that, as he had trade connections with his brother Philip, a merchant in Douglas, he may have been included in some of Philip Moore & Co's importations – over £10,900 value, placing them 15th on the overall list (see Table 2.1).

However, he did have several contacts in Liverpool. They appear to have been used mainly as a postal service - to forward his letters sent from the Island and to supply him not only with his return correspondence but also newspapers and magazines. One of these contacts was James Crosbie, who was involved in the Guinea trade. Moore wrote to him in March 1753 about a trunk containing 80 pieces of bandanoes, which had been sent from Liverpool on the *Molly*, John Moore master [no relation].[66] This letter suggests that the bandanoes were for Moore's use and not part of a cargo that a Crosbie vessel was to collect (see Chapter 3). There is some evidence that William, son of James Coul of Peel, had been a mariner on board one of Crosbie's vessels. When Coul died, Moore was asked to inform his father that he had owed Crosbie & Co £4 8s 8d, 'which they freely forgive'.[67]

When Crosbie died in 1755, Moore wrote to his son, that this would be 'a loss in general to his friends and [his] family in particular, with whom I heartily sympathise'.[68] John Frissel of Ramsey was appointed as the Crosbie family attorney on the Island to 'recover certain debts' due from James Watson of Ramsey. Frissel was one of the major importers of Guinea goods – over £7,150 worth. This connection with the Crosbies suggests that Frissel may have supplied their Guinea vessels with cargoes – at Ramsey. There were further family links with the Crosbies. John's brother, Henry, was a slave captain (see Appendix 5). He was also master of the *Isabella*, owned by James Crosbie and John Joseph Bacon.[16] But this vessel was not in the Guinea trade.

By the time Moore was concerned about the enlargement of Peel harbour, his contacts in Liverpool were William Haliday & Thomas Dunbar. Haliday's *Swallow* was captained by Thomas Bridson for part of her third voyage, when she was not in the Guinea trade, and Thomas Cubbin for her fourth and last voyage, in the trade once more.[16] Finally Moore corresponded with Robert Kennish, a former Manx master now settled in Liverpool. This correspondence was of a more domestic nature.

Douglas Harbour Bridge

Thomas Heywood of Nunnery Howe proposed that a bridge should be built across Douglas harbour to link his property with the main town. Developing the south side of Douglas harbour had several advantages. The town was expanding rapidly and 'ground is excessively wanted for all the purposes of trade'. Cellar and storehouse rents at Douglas were dearer than in Dublin. A street from the harbour mouth to the new bridge would add an area equal to 'one half of the present town'. Heywood would provide 'gratis' twenty-one feet of his harbour frontage for a public quay. If every purchaser 'whose lot of ground adjoins the harbour' also built a quay at their own expense, this would double the number of berths available for shipping.[69]

Heywood anticipated that the cost of building the bridge would be covered by subscriptions from the 'principal merchants' in Douglas. Some of the Douglas inhabitants, however, were 'apprehensive' that the bridge would result in several of these merchants moving to the southside of the town where they would build warehouses and 'mansion houses', so reducing the rents income of the 'native' landowners. 'For these and such like private self interested reasons, this good and public work hath been hitherto opposed and frustrated'.

Figure 5.2: George Moore's Plan of Douglas Harbour, 1757

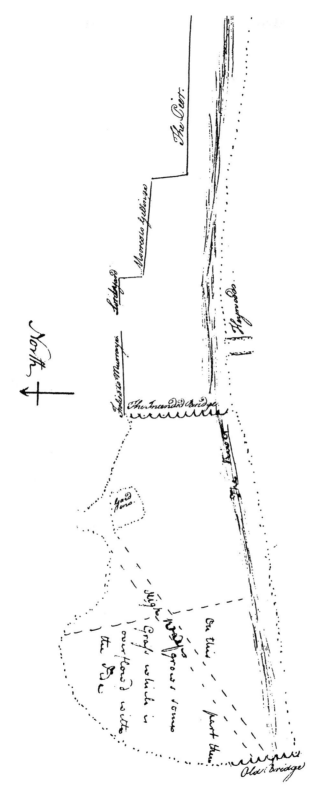

35

In September 1757 Heywood in person presented a memorial about the bridge to the Duke of Atholl in Scotland. He suggested that the Duke might make a small financial contribution towards the bridge fund. This would be 'a great means to encourage the work'. The Duke was somewhat wary about any financial commitment as then 'all other public works may expect the assistance of the Lord'.[70] The Harbour Committee (see below) met on 5 October 1757 and reported that the proposed bridge 'would not prejudice the harbour provided that one of the arches ... be built wide and capacious enough to be taken down and made a drawbridge, if the trade of the town shall hereafter require the harbour to be enlarged or extended'.[71]

The Moores's Intervention

In October 1757 George and Philip Moore petitioned Governor Cochrane because they were concerned about the 'animosities' over the intended bridge developing amongst the masters of vessels using the harbour: 'some of them being for a bridge, and others, by far the greatest number of them, being for no bridge'. If the bridge were built the captains opposed to it would 'circulate their opinion of the harbour being cramped and confined ... and probably magnify the danger and insufficiency'. This would 'terrify the African ships belonging to Liverpool and Lancaster' so that they would stop using the harbour, and the Island, for their Guinea cargoes.

There were already problems with the harbour, however, and, unless some action were taken to improve it, the merchants in the African trade would 'begin to entertain an opinion that sufficient public care is not enough taken of the harbour ... for the safety of their vessels trading to Douglas. It may lead them to imbibe a distaste of the harbour and incline them to remove their trade to some other harbour in this Isle or perhaps revive their inclination of having a floating factory established useful to supply their African cargoes with Dutch commodities'. The consequence of this would be 'alike injurious to his Grace the Duke of Atholl and to that valuable branch of trade in Douglas.'[72] No clear evidence has been found for this 'floating factory'.

The Moores suggested that an alternative, less expensive, solution which would also double the number of berths available would be to develop the harbour inland (see Figure 5.2).

The Liverpool and Lancaster Reactions

In parallel with the petition to Governor Cochrane, George Moore forewarned the Mayor of Liverpool about the consequences of the proposed bridge. The minutes of the Liverpool Town Council for this period do not appear to contain any reference to the subsequent discussion. Moore's comments might be 'as has been insinuated' a result of 'improper prejudices or party disputes'. In this case the merchants of Liverpool would be 'far from interesting ourselves at all in such disputes or showing the least bypass to either party'. If, however, the bridge would really 'affect the navigation of the harbour' then they would be very concerned about 'a matter of so great consequence to the trade and interest of this port'.

As they did not have enough information about the present harbour, or the planned changes, the Mayor and thirty other Liverpool merchants wrote to the Duke requesting 'a proper plan and survey ... particularly showing the nature of the ground and the depth of water both at spring and neap tides'. This plan would then help them to 'clear up our doubts concerning this affair'.[73]

An analysis of the Guinea vessels owned by all the signatories of this letter (see Fig 5.3), to the end of 1758 shows that they co-owned over 170 vessels, which undertook more than 340 Guinea voyages.[16] While it is not suggested that each one of these vessels called at the Isle of Man on every voyage, some of the names do appear in Appendix 2.

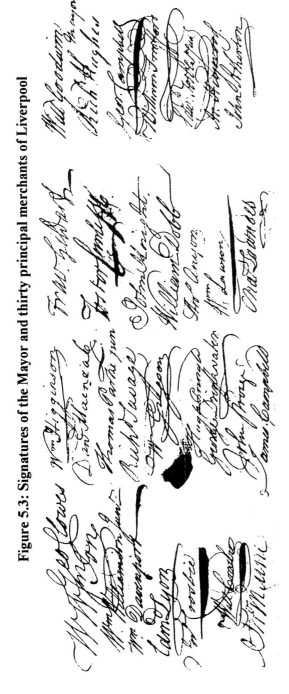

Figure 5.3: Signatures of the Mayor and thirty principal merchants of Liverpool

On 23 November 1757 the Duke reassured the Mayor: 'No permission shall be given for a bridge to be built on any part of the harbour of Douglas that may be prejudicial to the trade in general or more in particular to the town of Liverpool, for which corporation I have a very great regard'.[74]

When Robert Boyd, captain of the *Betty*, a Liverpool Guinea vessel, visited Peel, George Moore 'took the opportunity' of asking him about the bridge. Having discovered that Boyd was against the bridge, Moore asked for a written copy of his comments 'which he told me he would give in writing and consult with whatever commanders of Liverpool and Lancaster ships were at that time in Douglas.' A statement from these captains was forwarded to the Duke on 5 December 1757.

'[We] hereby give it as our opinions, in which we are joined by all the other several commanders of ships belonging to the ports whereunto we respectively belong, and with whom we have conversed, that the harbour of Douglas will be injured by the construction of any bridge built across it. That it is at present greatly insufficient for the trade resorting there and instead of lessening or contracting the harbour by a bridge it would be of the greatest benefit to have it six times larger. Our acquaintance with and particular knowledge of the harbour makes us with the greater certainty of the premises hereunto subscribe our hands'.

The signatories were: Robert Boyd; William Heyes of the *Judith* of Liverpool; James Carruthers of the *Shaw Perfect* of Liverpool and John Preston of the snow *Minerva* of Lancaster.[75]

In the meantime the proposed bridge continued to be a subject in the correspondence between Governor Cochrane and the Duke. On 7 December 1757 the Governor wrote: 'As for the bridge at Douglas there is nothing but interest and humour that makes the opposition and when the merchants of Liverpool are acquainted with a true state of the affair their objections will cease'.[76]

The Duke's response was: 'I find there is great heats on both sides, and as in such cases it is much better and safer to forbear carrying a thing into execution than remove objections against it when it is done'. He had received two further letters from George and Philip Moore. 'I cannot help thinking that these Moores are rather too busy in this affair of a bridge at Douglas'.[77] On 2 October 1758 the Duke reported to Francis Gildart, Town Clerk of Liverpool that the suggested survey had been completed. 'I find by my governor ... (who is now here) that it is agreed a bridge should be built as it plainly appears it can in no respect be a detriment to the navigation of the river and Port of Douglas'.[78]

Peel Harbour
Both George and Philip Moore had campaigned against the building of Heywood's bridge at Douglas. George Moore now campaigned with even more determination for the development of Peel harbour so that it would be 'commodious' for the Guinea vessels.

Peel harbour had two advantages over Douglas: it was 'extremely convenient to the North Channel through which is found a convenient passage in time of war to America and Africa for the Liverpool ships, the Lancaster and Whitehaven ships'[79] and it could be used by vessels when because of the wind they could not get into Douglas harbour.

In January 1758 Moore told Haliday & Dunbar that there were three Guinea ships in Peel bay which had intended to go to Douglas 'to take on board part of their cargoes. They left Liverpool with a south-east wind and blowing fresh. When they came to this Island they were afraid to look into the bay or run into the harbour of Douglas so for safety came round to this part of the Isle and it's a pity to see them riding in our bay waiting their goods coming from Douglas. Had their goods been in this town they would speedily have been shipped and the ships by this time clear of the coast of Ireland with a south east wind'.[80] Four vessels had sailed from Liverpool between 30 December 1757 and 6 January 1758. The *Dahomey*, Thomas Nichols captain, ran ashore in Douglas harbour. The vessel bulged and in February 1758 her cargo was returned to Liverpool on board the *Douglas Packet*. The other three vessels, possibly those in Peel harbour, were the *Whydah*, Chris Ewings captain, the *Prince Tom*, Charles Cooke and the *Royal Family*, Wilson Shepherd.[16]

In March 1759 the *Upton*, Thomas Birch captain, was also in Peel bay, waiting for her Guinea cargo to be forwarded from Douglas. Moore had 'frequently the pleasure' of seeing Birch, who told him that his owner was James Gildart of Liverpool. When Moore asked Birch why the Guinea vessels did not use Peel, he replied that one reason might be that the Liverpool merchants had 'no acquaintance' in the town. A letter was instantly sent to Gildart offering Moore's 'best services in the care of any kind of goods you occasionally might order the landing of here or in the supply of any commodities wherein I deal'. No evidence has been found that Gildart did send any of his vessels to Moore for supplies.

The *Upton* stayed in Peel bay 'for some days with a heavy gale and easterly winds and on its moderating, being tired waiting, he set sail and reached Ramsey Bay, where he writes me he met the goods from Douglas'.[81] Birch had spent £12 at Peel – his payment was credited to Moore's account by Haliday & Dunbar.[82]

The following month, Thomas Rumbold & Co's vessel the *Hare*, George Colley captain, was in Peel bay also because of a south-east wind which had 'forced' him to leave Douglas. Colley 'seemed very much concerned about the disappointment and regretted that he must stay [at the island] with so fair a wind to proceed on his voyage'. Moore was asked if he could supply the *Hare* with the necessary goods. On 25 May 1759 'some brandy and other goods for the coast of Guinea' valued at over £160 were put on board and 'in the evening he set sail with a favourable wind which this day continues'.[83]

Peel harbour had its own problems: lack of water except at high tide and lack of space both within the harbour itself and on the quay. Because of the lack of water, the harbour was 'not at all convenient' for laden vessels due to discharge there. It had only 9 to 10 feet of water even in an ordinary spring tide so that vessels drawing 10 to 13 feet water still could not get into the harbour and if they arrived on a neap tide 'the difficulty and the danger become increased'.[84] As it was on the west side of the Island, Peel suffered from difficulties when the wind was favourable for Douglas.

Figure 5.4 George Moore's Scheme for the Enlargement of Peel Harbour

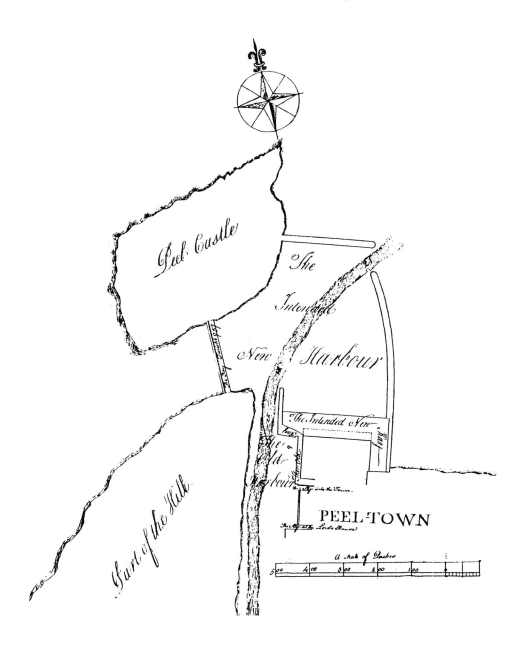

Moore drew up a scheme for enlarging the harbour (see Figure 5.4). The next stage was to raise the necessary funds, which were estimated as £1,500. Moore canvassed every Liverpool merchant who went to the Island. John Maine, William Boats and James Clemens all visited Peel. Boats and Clemens 'seemed to be unanimously of opinion in respect of the intended improvement and Mr Boats thought it merited all assistance'.[85] A month later Moore was able to report 'Captain Clemens I find continues in his opinion of the great utility of the intended improvement of this harbour'[86]. Maine was not quite so forthcoming: 'By three or four opportunities from Liverpool since you were here, I had letters but as I have not been favoured with any from you ... I shall be glad of a line from you as it would please me to know what are the public sentiments with you in respect of our intended harbour'.[87]

The plan was that Peel should raise £500 from subscription and that the remaining £1,000 should be borrowed at Liverpool, where Moore managed to negotiate an interest rate of 5%, which was 1% less than on the Island. The security for this loan would be the harbour dues, which were paid by all the shipping using the Peel anchorage.

Traditionally the harbours had funded their own repairs from the fees they collected, or by way of a loan from the Island's Harbour Fund. As a matter of courtesy, Moore wrote to the Duke, explaining what was planned. 'If this port was rendered commodious it would not only be inviting for the ships of [Liverpool, Lancaster or Whitehaven] ... but would also be inviting to the ships belonging to the Clyde and with them point a pass to a new branch of trade with the merchants of Glasgow with whom at present your Isle has little or no trade excepting in the tobacco way'.[88]

The reply was dated 8 March 1759: 'if the Governor and Officers report their approbation to the scheme, you may be sure my Lord Duke will most willingly concur. If a thing of this kind were to take place, His Grace thinks the sooner it is set about the better'. Encouraged by this, Moore ordered a load of timber, which would cost £100.

He had not realised that his proposal would be opposed by the Governor, Basil Cochrane, who placed every imaginable hurdle in Moore's path: the application had to be referred to the Harbour Committee and then to the House of Keys, where it was rejected in favour of developments at other ports on the Island.

In July 1799 the 'inhabitants of Peeltown and its vicinity' put forward a familiar-sounding memorial to the Duke of Atholl, recommending the enlargement of Peel harbour. The argument had changed, however, because Revestment had intervened. Now the case was based on Peel's advantages for the herring fishing.[89]

6

Back on the Island

Hugh Cosnahan imported Guinea goods into Douglas – he was one of the merchants who supplied the William Davenport vessels (see Appendix 2.5a). He was also deeply involved in the running trade. Rum was one of the main items of that trade and it is clear from the customs entries that some of this rum was landed on the Island by Guinea vessels on their way back to their home ports. The Guinea trade therefore also supported smuggling.

There are two, apparently irreconcilable, impressions of Cosnahan as a man. He married Ellinor Finch and they had fifteen children, only six of whom survived into adulthood. John turned to politics while both James and Mark became merchants. One of the three daughters, Catherine, married George Moore's son John and, after his death, James Wilks the collector of customs at Castletown. Brother-in-law Michael Finch was a Liverpool Guinea vessel captain and co-owner. When he died in 1775 his 'trusty and well-beloved friend' Cosnahan became supervisor and guardian of his children. In a deed of gift dated 1792 Philip Finch assigned to his 'loving son-in-law' the Lough (sic) estate at Kirk Conchan (see Figure 6.1 below) and several other properties in Douglas. In his own right Cosnahan purchased Ballafletcher and Larkhill farms in Braddan parish and he also owned Kew, where he took the family for the summer. He has been described as 'a man of persuasive eloquence' and the 'darling' of the House of Keys, of which he was a member from 1777 to his death in 1799.[90]

Figure 6.1: Douglas and Loch House

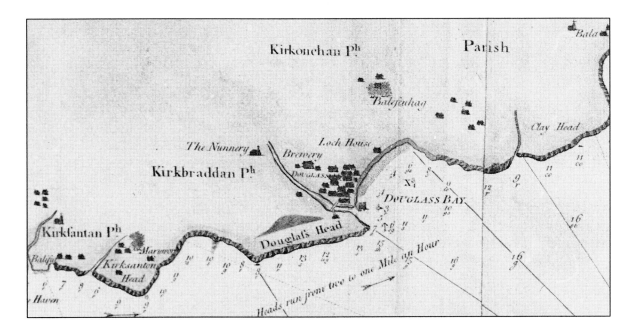

As will be seen, this does not correspond with the impression obtained from Cosnahan's long and complaining correspondence with George Moore, mainly over outstanding debts, or his apparently desperate attempts to obtain a government position.

After the Revestment Act of 1765 the Isle of Man could no longer be used as an entrepôt for Guinea goods. The slave traders looked elsewhere and inevitably the cost of the Guinea cargoes would have increased for those who were previously supplied by way of the Island. The smuggling trade also suffered. On the other hand, it is highly likely that, considering the large number of business failures before 1765, there would have been a change in the pattern of trade anyway.

With Revestment several merchants left the Island to ply their trade elsewhere. Cosnahan was one of those who stayed: 'I have been a struggler in business here since the year 1765 without success but on the contrary have lost several thousand pounds in the fish trade that has hurt me much.'[91] The development of the fishing industry, to supply the Guinea trade and the Plantations with provisions, was one of the many post-Revestment possibilities.

Back on the Island
According to the Liverpool Trade and Shipping database, a few of the Guineamen called at the Island on their homeward voyages.[16] One example is the *Rebecca*, Robert Boyd captain, which was reported 'at the Isle of Man' in 1759. The Manx customs entries also record the presence of Guinea vessels at the Island on their way back from the West Indies, Virginia etc, and from Africa. These records indicate that they either landed parts of their homeward cargoes or returned some of their Guinea goods, which would have been seized had they been taken back to the home port, and could have been identified as coming originally from the 'Isleman'.

Over twenty Guinea vessels have been identified as landing cargoes on the Island from the 'Americas' [America and the West Indies]. While the majority of these vessels then returned to Liverpool, six of them went to Lancaster, one to Whitehaven and it is believed that another, the *Thistle*, would have returned to Kirkcudbright. Not only do these vessels close the 'triangle' in terms of the Island's involvement in the Guinea trade but also they provide additional information about the cargoes that were purchased with money from the sale of the slaves.

<u>Rum, brown sugar, coffee and rice</u>
Rum was a major importation into the Island. As Governor Cochrane wrote to the Duke of Atholl in 1756: 'We have had of late a glorious time and great many ships arrived with rum etc. and to my great surprise all our ships has escaped the many privateers that are now on the seas'.[92] George Moore owned two vessels, the *Peggy* and the *Lilly*, which were constantly employed in the rum trade. Robert Arthur's vessel the *Kingston* also brought rum to the Island – on one occasion in partnership with Moore. Other Scottish merchants warehoused supplies of rum at Douglas and Peel. These were decanted into small casks and then awaited the Manx or Irish wherries which were to run them on to the coasts of the Irish Sea, preferably on a 'dark night of the moon'.

The amounts of rum landed from the Guinea vessels vary from a few gallons to several tons. The names of the merchants receiving this rum on the Island are known – and so are their smuggling links. Once it arrived the rum tended to become intermingled with that brought directly through the West Indian trade. It should be possible, however, to trace the origins of some of the rum delivered to customers in Scotland from the importation of Guinea goods into the Isle of Man to the vessel that landed the rum on the Island and the wherries which transported it to the Scottish coast.[93]

Table 6.1: Guinea Vessels landing Rum, Sugar & Rice on the Isle of Man

Date	Vessel	Master	From	Goods	Merchant
1741	*St George*	John Buchan	Barbados	Rum	William Murray
1745	*Worcester*	William Harrison	Barbados	Rum	Benjamin Perry
1749	*Jolly Batchelor*	Edward Freeman	Antigua	Rum	William Teare & Edward Freeman
1749	*Molly*	Phil Styth	Barbados	Rum	Thomas Pennington
1752	*Betty*	Samuel Sacheverell	Barbados	Rum	William Murray
1752	*Thomas*	Patrick Allen	Barbados	Rum	William Teare
1755	*Ferrett*	Thomas Whitehead	St Kitts	Rum	John Berry
1756	*Thomas*	Daniel Hayes	Barbados	Rum	Daniel Hayes
1756	*Swallow*	William Oard	Barbados	Rum & sugar	Philip Moore & Co
1757	*Lowther*	John Houseman	Barbados	Rum & sugar	Philip Moore & Co
1758	*Expedition*	Duncan Campbell	St Croix	Rum	William Teare & James Grayburn
1758	*Sally*	John Thompson	St Kitts	Rum & sugar	Philip Moore & Co
1759	*Vianna*	William Hutton	Jamaica	Rum, sugar & coffee	William Hutton, Thomas Quayle & Jacob Abraham
1759	*Lively*	John Giball	Montserrat	Rum	Paul Bridson & William Teare
1761	*Young James*	Robert Mitchell	Jamaica	Rum	Abraham Vianna
1762	*Prince Vada*	John Clifton	St Kitts	Sugar	John Clifton
1762	*Prince George*	Daniel Baynes	Jamaica	Coffee	John Joseph Bacon
1762	*Marquis of Granby*	Robert Dodson	Jamaica	Rice & sugar	Thomas Stephen

Some of the Manx merchants were involved in more than one of these rum importations. Philip Moore & Co of Douglas imported rum and brown sugar on three Lancaster vessels: in August 1756 on the *Swallow*, William Oard captain, from Barbados, 6 May 1757 the *Lowther*, John Houseman, also from Barbados and August 1758 the *Sally*, John Thompson, from St Kitts.

Figure 6.2: The Lancaster Trade

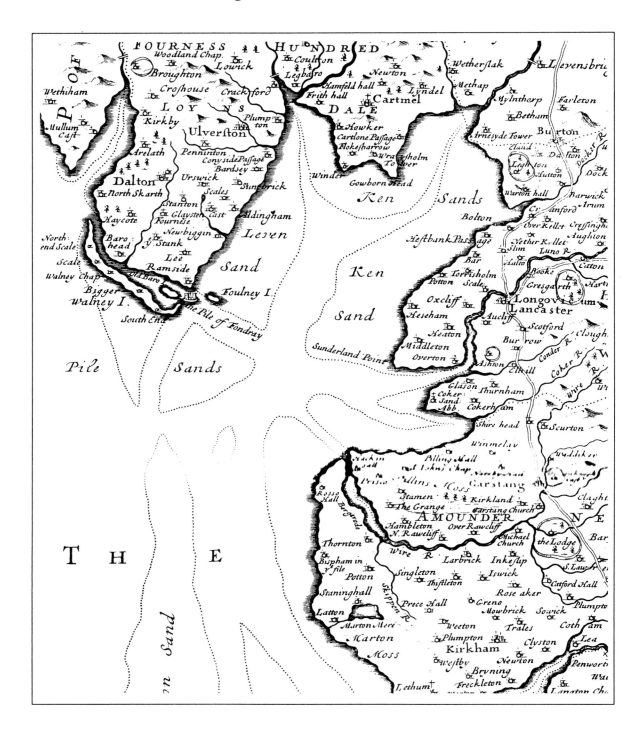

44

Similarly William Teare imported rum on three of the Liverpool Guineamen. Of these the *Thomas* was owned by a group of merchants based in Barbados, the *Lively* by John Knight, Chris Davenport et al and the *Expedition* by Richard Oswald and John Mill.[16] The Oswald & Mill presence provides another link with Scotland. Originally Scottish merchants, they moved to London from where they ran a successful slaving business.[94] Their vessel the *Expedition* appears more than once in the Manx records. John Tear was captain on two of the voyages and one of the mariners who died on board was a Manxman.

Abraham Vianna was one of the co-owners of the *Vianna* (see Appendix 4). He did not import any of her rum: the merchants involved were Thomas Quayle and Jacob Abraham [often referred to as 'Abraham the Jew' and a known supplier of rum to David Dunlop & Co, the smugglers of Loans in Ayrshire] and the master, William Hutton. Vianna did land rum from Jamaica on the *Young James*, Robert Mitchell captain.

John Joseph Bacon imported 1,568 lbs weight of coffee on a Whitehaven Guinea vessel, the *Prince George*, Daniel Baynes captain. Bacon's activities have proved elusive. He was clearly involved in the Guinea trade: fourth on the list of those importing Guinea goods and co-owner of twelve Liverpool registered vessels, five of which were slavers (see Appendix 4). Yet so far little hard information has been found about his activities.

William Teare was one of the merchants who appear to have imported rum purchased from sale of slaves but delivered to the Island on a vessel that was not in the Guinea trade. There are at least five vessels in this category:[16]

Date	Vessel	Master	From	Guineaman	Master
1748	*Judith*	John Simmons	Antigua	*Ann Galley*	John Simmons
1749	*Martin*	William Hayes	Barbados	*Chesterfield*	John Jenkins
1752	*Elizabeth*	Nathaniel Sayers	New London	*Barbados Merchant*	John Wilson
1753	*Expedition*	William Campbell	Barbados	*Thomas & Martha*	John Gillman
1758	*Fanny*	Edward Ashburner	Barbados	*Blackburne*	John Perkin

In each case the two vessels shared at least one common owner. John Simmons, captain of the *Ann Galley*, brought home the *Judith* himself.

John Tarleton's Rum
According to his accounts, John Tarleton IV lodged rum on the Island in the hands of both Paul Bridson and Philip Moore & Co. On 13 June 1756 Tarleton noted that Paul Bridson owed him £285 16s 10d. By 1758 the total was £486 12s 10d and by 1762 £2724. In 1763 there is a reference to 'Rum at the Isle of Man in Bridson's hands' valued at £3044. In his annual accounts dated 30 April 1775 Tarleton has a subheading of 'Bad and dubious debts'. Philip Moore with Paul Bridson & Son and Paul Bridson & Son on their own are bracketed together and described as 'dishonest men'.[95] This is a somewhat sad ending to the Tarleton connection with the Isle of Man through the Guinea trade, which had started in 1719.

No records have been found of any Tarleton Guinea vessels calling at the Island, let alone at the appropriate dates. Bridson did import rum on Tarleton's West India trade vessels: the *Lucy*, Nicholas Boulton master in 1754, the *Bridget*, Samuel Lay in 1755, the *John*, Nicholas Boulton in 1756, all from Santa Cruz, and on the *Fanny* with Edward Ashburner master from Barbados in 1758 (see above).

Tobacco

Andrew Bermingham, who ran a tobacco manufactory in Douglas, imported tobacco from Virginia on the *Nancy* of Lancaster, John Watson captain, in 1753. Although the *Nancy* was a slaving vessel, it is not certain whether or not this importation related to a slaving voyage or to a direct one between Lancaster and Virginia.

Bermingham died in 1755 and attached to his will is an inventory of his tobacco business. This included a beam, scales and lead weights, 370 tobacco sheets, 4 lying tobacco presses, one small pigtail press, two standing press, three tables, six wheels, hobbies and spindles, a cutting engine, 30 lbs weight of tobacco cord, two casks of oil, a barrel of tar, a snuff mill with its utensils, 27 rolls of pigtail tobacco, 8,000 lbs leaf tobacco, 4 hundred weight of stem tobacco, 6,300 lbs roll tobacco, 413 lbs lugg tobacco, 145 rolls of tobacco in one pound rolls and 81 lbs of snuff. Many of these items were purchased by the Reeves brothers.

The importation from the *Nancy* is interesting because it was unusual for tobacco to be brought directly to the Island – most of these supplies were relanded there having been imported into Britain first and then sent to either Rotterdam or Norway. Direct links with the tobacco plantations in America are few. In 1741 the *Thomas*, Evan Jones captain, from Virginia did not land any tobacco but returned Guinea goods to the Island.

Returned Guinea goods (see Appendix 2.6)

It will be remembered that it was 'in contravention of the law' to collect East Indian goods from the Isle of Man: George Dow of the *Sincerity* revenue cruiser attempted to seize the *Hope* dogger because it was believed that she had these goods on board for merchants on the Island. William Davenport & Co were concerned in case Thomas Dickson unloaded any of the Isleman cargo at Cork and three of the vessels directed to go from the Island to Thomas Mears in 1763 were seized at Liverpool.

None of these goods could be returned to the home port – if they were both the vessel and the cargo were liable to seizure. Yet frequently the Guinea vessels would have some of the original cargo on board during the homeward voyage, and would off-load it on the Isle of Man.

Robert Boyd, captain of the *Rebecca*, returned from Senegal directly to the Isle of Man in 1759. According to the customs entries for 28 December Paul Bridson & Son imported 'from Africa': 1 puncheon & 3 cases of bafts, 4 chests of beads, 75 brass kettles and 50 brass pans valued at £361 13s 4d. Presumably there were no slaves on the coast and so Boyd felt that it was more appropriate to return straight home.

The *James*, William Sacheverell captain, only purchased 28 out of her complement of 60 slaves. On 20 September 1753 she landed with William Teare from Barbados a cask of beads and eleven assorted pieces of bejulapants, negrapants, tapseils, and silesias (see Appendix 3) with a total value of £13 12s 4d.

Finally there were the goods that had been damaged in transit and so made unsaleable (see Chapter 3 for a discussion of what eventually happened to these goods).

'Damnified' goods were landed on the Island from:

29 October 1751	*Thomas*, Pat Allen, from Barbados
14 September 1754	*Rainbow*, Robert Makin, from Barbados
16 August 1755	*Ryder*, John Sacheverell, from Africa

The Revestment Act 1765
Appendix 2 shows that at least 90 Guinea vessels had called at the Isle of Man – before 1765.

Although the purchase of the fiscal rights of Isle of Man from the Derbys and the Atholls had been contemplated by the English government for several years, the Revestment Act came as a considerable shock to several merchants on the Island. As Robert Arthur of Irvine wrote to James Oates at Douglas on 6 February 1765 'I believe it is now out of all doubt that the Isle is sold and it is said the Duke of Atholl is to get as an equivalent, or in part, the Duke of Perth's and another forfeited estate contiguous to it, which it's thought will be a good bargain, though a loss to numbers. The Duke has not acted up to what might have been expected from his promises. Had he been in want of money it might have apologised for him ... No doubt this will be attended with bad consequences ... there will doubtless be some time allowed for carrying off the goods that are on hand'.[96]

Arthur was correct in his supposition. The merchants were allowed to export to Liverpool, by licence, any Guinea goods imported before 1 March 1765. Hugh Cosnahan was one of the Manx merchants who used the licence system. He sent 1,820 hundred weight of gunpowder there.

Gunpowder
This 'Isleman' powder proceeded to flood the Liverpool market. Christopher Hasell reported regularly on the problem to Mark Nesfield, at his office in Broad Street, London. The imported gunpowder was lower priced: 72/- per barrel compared with the regular Liverpool prices of 87/6 and 80/- 'ready money'. In July 1765 Miles Barber had 'very near 2,000 barrels' of it, which he was selling at 70/- and 'I fancy he will lower it soon'. The price did lower: to 64/- in March 1766 and 62/- in April of that year, still holding the price in September. Unfortunately some of the Liverpool Guinea captains reckoned that the Isleman powder was 'as good as the London powder'. In the meantime the London powder appeared to deteriorate at a faster rate than that from the Island. It was 'much fuller of dust' and 'not of an even grain'. In addition the London powder was 'not near so strong'. In fact Hasell would 'as soon prefer the Isleman powder for my own ships as yours'.

William Boats showed some interest in Hasell's London gunpowder. He was prepared to purchase 100 barrels at 75/-. Hasell 'went down with him to the magazine along with his captain. But when we came to look at it his captain would not take it it was so dusty and lumpy but preferred the Isleman powder before it'. This situation continued until November 1766 when Hasell commented: 'I am apt to think they begin not to like the Isleman powder as Mr Miles Barber, who has some 100 barrels by him, bought 50 barrels off Mr Craven last week at 80/-.' At last, in November 1767, Hasell was able to report: 'I thought it was my duty to acquaint you that all the Isleman powder is sold some time since'.[97]

Duties owed to the Duke of Atholl
Cosnahan and John Taubman, were two of the Manx merchants who refused to pay the duty owed to the Duke of Atholl for the goods that could not be sent from the Island on the Guinea ships, or as part of the smuggling trade. These duties are shown in Figure 6.3 [it may be noticed that this includes a minor arithmetic error]. As Cosnahan explained, his refusal to pay was 'not from any intention of evading the payment' due to the Duke of Atholl. He had been away from the Island when the news about the Revestment Act arrived there and so had not been able to act as quickly as some of the other merchants. He still had a quantity of goods on hand that he 'did not know what to do with'.[98]

Figure 6.3: Duties 'refused' the Duke of Atholl

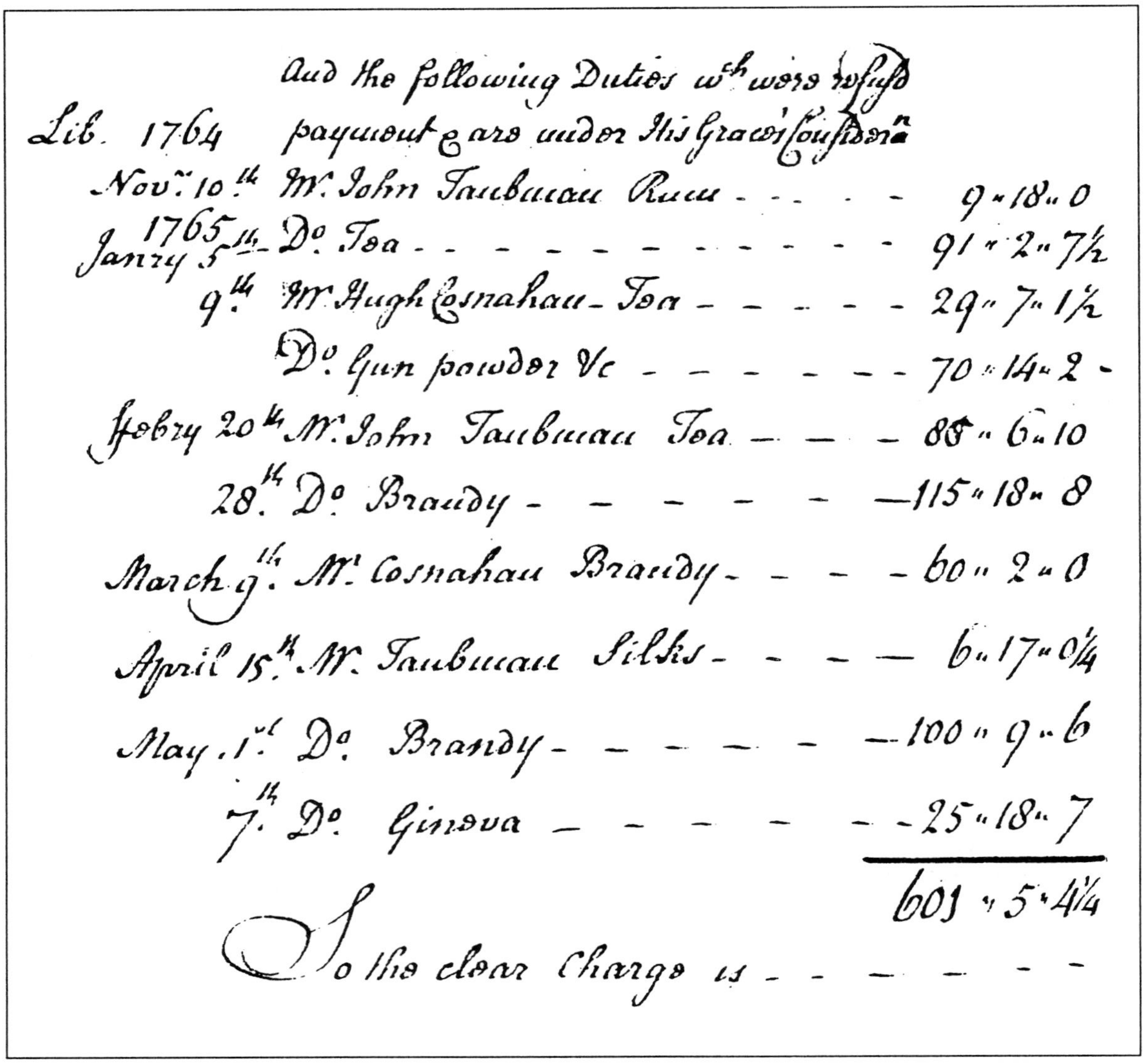

> And the following Duties w[ch] were refused
>
> Lib. 1764 payment & are under His Graces' Consideration
>
> Nov[r] 10th Mr. John Taubman Rum - - - - - 9 " 18 " 0
>
> 1765 Jan[ry] 5th D[o] Tea - - - - - - - - - - 91 " 2 " 7½
>
> 9th Mr. Hugh Cosnahan - Tea - - - - - 29 " 7 " 1½
>
> D[o] Gun powder &c - - - - - - 70 " 14 " 2 -
>
> Feb[ry] 20th Mr. John Taubman Tea — — - 88 " 6 " 10
>
> 28th D[o] Brandy - - - - - - —115 " 18 " 8
>
> March 9th Mr. Cosnahan Brandy - - - -60 " 2 " 0
>
> April 15th Mr. Taubman Silks - - — 6 " 17 " 0¼
>
> May 1st D[o] Brandy - - - - - —100 " 9 " 6
>
> 7th D[o] Ginova — - - - - -25 " 18 " 7
>
> 601 " 5 " 4¼
>
> So the clear Charge is - - - - - - - -

Cosnahan owed £160 5s. In the past he had paid 'several thousand pounds duty' to the Dukes of Atholl 'ever cheerfully' and he was 'never once out of the way' when called on to go to Castletown to pay what was owed 'nor made two payments of one demand'. Now he felt that the duties should not be charged because in other countries where imported goods were merely warehoused ready for exportation no duties were payable. He hoped the Duke would take the case 'into your humane consideration and not insist upon the duties demanded for the above goods that I have sent to Liverpool'.[99] In 1766 the Duke suggested a solution – to remit £50 of the duties, so reducing the bill to £110 5s. Cosnahan's response, in writing, was that he did not propose to pay the Duke any duties.[100]

Taubman owed £435 15s 9d in duty. He wrote to Dan Mylrea and John Quayle, now the Duke's stewards, 'I am really sorry to be under the disagreeable necessity of telling you that I think it extremely hard, that I should be charged with the duties for the following and other good reasons: You are no strangers to the manner in which the trading people of this place were treated, who instead of having an intimation or advice of what was proposed or intended in respect of this Island were amused and even assured by you, Mr Quayle, in a public manner, that their excellencies the late Lord and Lady of this Isle had not the least intention or design to part with or dispose of the Isle, though it now appears that it was actually then in treaty'.[101]

As a result of these reassurances, Taubman had been 'induced' to make considerable importations. No sooner had these arrived, than to his 'great surprise' Taubman discovered that the Atholls had 'concluded a bargain' with the British government over the future of the Island. This had not taken into proper consideration the stocks of goods and merchandise already imported and warehoused, as would have been done had the Island been a 'conquered country'. As a result, Taubman had 'really sustained many considerable losses and may yet be greatly affected and injured in my prosperity'.

Mr Hammersley, the Duke's legal representative in London, proposed that Cosnahan, Taubman and others should be prosecuted in the Manx courts for their duties. 'But the delays, difficulties and hazard only confirm us in our former opinion, that England is the properest place to bring them to justice'. There was another reason for moving any prosecutions away from the Island. 'Were your Grace sensible of the present disposition of the people and circumstances of affairs in this Isle, we flatter ourselves that your Grace would approve of our interfering either with the Government or people as little as possible'.[102]

After Revestment
In 1799 Captain Small wrote a memorandum about the Duke of Atholl's affairs in the Isle of Man. He suggested trying to bring the African trade back to the Island.

> '*The Liverpool merchants in the Guinea trade are at present under the necessity of sending to Holland and to Guernsey for their spirits and trinkets necessary for carrying on their African trade. If the people of the Isle of Man who export herrings to the Mediterranean were allowed to import beads from Venice, and spirits of all kinds from Holland and France, to be lodged in the King's warehouse, and to be delivered to the Liverpool merchants under bond that it was not to be landed in any part of Great Britain or Ireland but only employed in their African trade, it would make a great increase in the revenue of the Island: and besides it would be an amazing advantage to the inhabitants at large, as it would bring the Liverpool ships to Douglas, by which means more money would circulate among the country people, who could furnish these vessels with fresh provisions, at the same time that it would be the means of increasing the harbour dues, which in time might produce a fund for enlarging it, as well as for the beginning of one for building a dock. It is to be presumed that the Liverpool merchants would support an application to Parliament upon this subject, as from the best information it is supposed that it would save them annually no less a sum than £30,000: and moreover after they have for some time been in the habit of frequenting the harbour of Douglas, its superior advantages to their own would soon occur to them and its being a better outlet to the Atlantic ocean than any other harbour in the Irish Channel, they might in turn see the advantages of wintering*

in Douglas Harbour, and the proposal of building a dock would naturally come from themselves'.[38]

However, the abolition movement was in full swing by this stage and the Guinea trade was abolished in 1807.

<u>Hugh Cosnahan's Problems</u>
Cosnahan's refusal to pay his duties appears to have been due to the serious financial situation that was developing. Figure 6.4 shows the extreme lengths he went to in order to emphasise the severity of his position – his reply to George Moore is written on the cover of the letter sent to him by Moore, whose writing can be easily identified.

The result of the Reeves brothers 'failing' in business was described in Chapter 4. Cosnahan was also owed £110 4s by Philip Moore, George Moore's son. Phil was no longer on the Island and in July 1776 Cosnahan wrote to Moore 'It's in my opinion more reasonable that you should be in advance than I should want to serve a growing family. If my son owed you and I able to pay you I declare I should'.[103] The correspondence between Cosnahan and Moore continued for another seven years. Finally, in February 1783, Moore agreed that he would pay the debt, in London, although Cosnahan would have preferred the money on the Island 'having occasion for such at present'.[104] Throughout this correspondence Cosnahan had not told Moore that the £110 4s 2d was the balance owing when accounts were settled between him and Phil on 31 December 1763. In the meantime, on 8 February 1772, Cosnahan had furnished Phil Moore with another account, adding interest @ 5% for 7 years 9 months and 7 days i.e. £42 15s 7d. This had increased the principal sum. The additional interest @ 5% to 31 December 1782, a further 10 years, 10 months and 23 days added another £83 4s 2d. Moore was clearly incensed.

Cosnahan replied: 'If you had asked me ... how his account stood on my books I should have stated it so, but as you only required how much it was when he left this Island so I complied ... I beg you may not take this amiss as I really and truly do not mean to give any or the least offence'.[105] At this somewhat late stage Moore checked son Phil's account book and found a charge of £18 10s against Cosnahan for an eighth share in the *George*, which had been co-owned by Phil, James Oates of Douglas and. John Maine of Liverpool. Twenty years afterwards, Cosnahan could find no record of his involvement in the ship. 'Possibly such might have happened between him [Phil] and James Oates, who might have meant me a concern and that I might have said I would not for ten guineas hold such from which I presume the charge must have been made but I am at present as greater stranger to it as the child unborn. When I see Mr Oates I shall make enquiry about it and shall be glad he may clear it up'.[106]

Oates did remember 'something of a vessel called the *George* commanded by Edward McGill, an old ship mate of mine, and who I recommended to the late John Maine ... Mr P Moore had also an interest in a Guineaman John Clinton (sic) Commander in which vessel Mr Bacon was concerned'.[107] This was the *Prince Vada*. It is the only record that has been found of Phil's direct involvement in the Guinea trade (see Appendix 4).

Cosnahan also tried to obtain an official post on the Island, to give himself a fixed income. In May 1789 he contacted George Farquhar in Edinburgh. 'When you was last in this place I much wished for an opportunity of having a little <u>private and confidential</u> talk with you... I meant to have requested the favour of you to solicit His Grace for his interest in some suitable employment and the Government in this Island'. Cosnahan had wanted the Water Bailiff's post but that was 'conferred on the worthy man George Savage [son of Pat Savage, Guinea goods importer of Peel] which I am not sorry for'. Now the Island's Collector of

Customs, Richard Betham, was 'not well and in a declining state. If he should be shortly called away doubtless there will not want applications to succeed him'. However, Cosnahan could guarantee that 'I should give satisfaction to my benefactor and to Government, though a Manxman'.[108] On 31 May 1789 Betham 'paid the debt of nature'[109]. The post of Collector was given to another 'worthy gentleman', Captain Small.

Figure 6.4: Hugh Cosnahan to George Moore, 2 September 1766

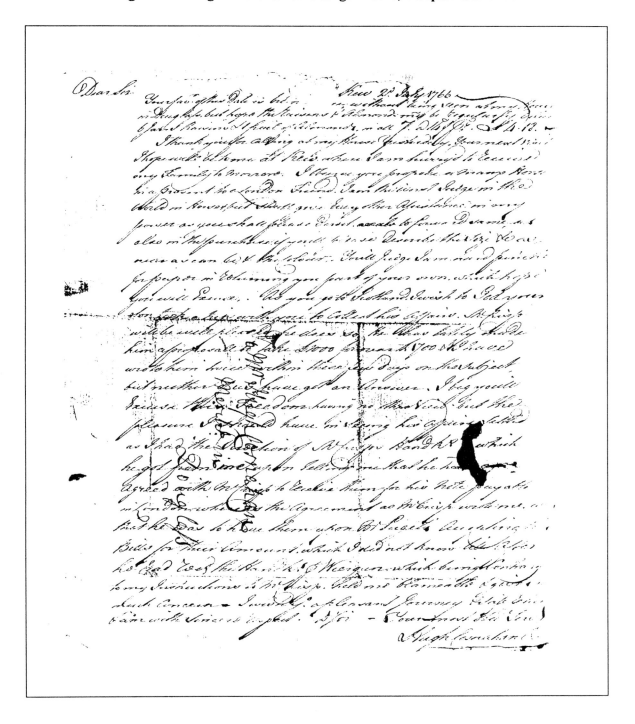

Archibald Hamilton, the Island's comptroller 'who resides in London' was planning to resign. He had planned 'to get a brother or a nephew appointed in his berth but that His Grace of Atholl prevented it'. However, Hamilton's nephew was appointed. The only remaining vacancy was that of barrack master at Castletown, replacing the late Robert Lightfoot. 'If such should or any new appointment that would be a livelihood to a family I would still be urging you my friend to throw in your word in my behalf'.[110]

When Cosnahan died in 1799 he left his estates to his son John and each of the other five children received between £200 and £250. This does not tally with the picture of his financial state described in the previous pages.

This ends the section about the Guinea trade as it affected people living on the Isle of Man. It should be emphasised that it was just that, trade. Importations of goods from a Dutch vessel could include tea for the smuggling trade as well as East India goods to be collected by a Guinea vessel from Liverpool, Whitehaven or Lancaster. Rum imported into the Island might have come from the West India trade as easily as from a Guinea voyage. It is doubtful whether the customers for the rum in Scotland were told whether it came from the sale of Glasgow manufactories or of slaves in the West Indies.

The next section looks at the ownership of Liverpool Guinea vessels and at the Manx mariners on board the slave ships.

Off the Isle of Man

John Cowle, who had been on board a Guinea vessel before he was impressed into the navy, wrote this letter to his brother, who was still on the Island:

'Dear Brother,

I hope you'll have a little more sense in your head than to offer to go to sea but stay at home and enjoy the fruits of your labour on shore. There was several pressed when I was and preferred to enter as volunteers.

John Cowle
HMS Superb at Spithead, 1779'

Cowle was one of the hundreds of Manx mariners who sought their 'fortunes' at sea and who became a part of the Guinea trade. In this instance little is known about Cowle's maritime career, but a great deal is known about other Manx mariners.

This section of the book concentrates on the Manx who were involved in the Guinea trade away from the Island – as co-owners of slaving vessels or as their captains and crew. It is based on six very different sources of information:

- the Liverpool Shipping & Trade database,
- Hugh Crow's *Memoirs* and other information about the Triangular voyages,
- the Minutes of Evidence before a select committee of the House of Commons, appointed on 29 January 1790,
- the Remarks on the voyage of the *Ranger*, John Corran captain, in 1789 and 1790,
- the Journal of the voyage of the *Duke of Argyle*, John Newton captain, in 1750 and 1751 and
- an account by Charles Christian, surgeon on board the *William*, Richard Hart captain, in 1800 and 1801.

With the exception of some of the Hugh Crow extracts, the section is largely illustrated from previously unpublished material.

Figure 7.1: Africa and the Guinea Coast

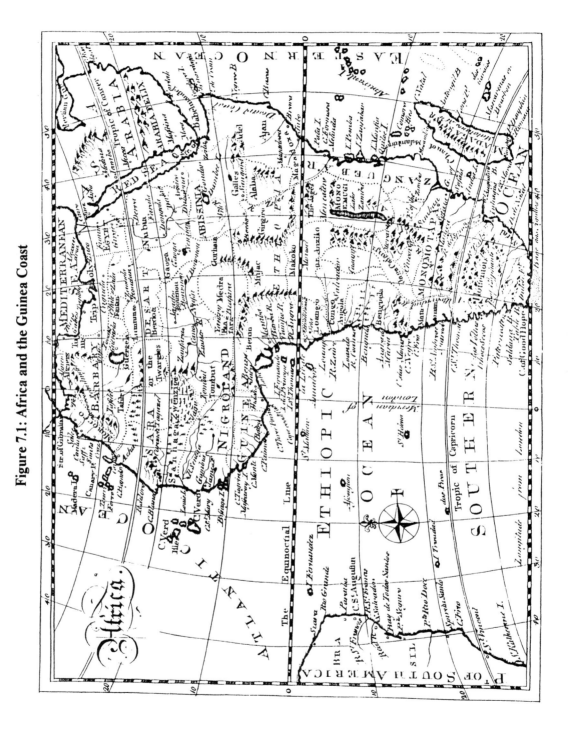

7

Manx Partnerships in Liverpool Guinea Vessels
1744-1786

[signature: Robt Kennedy]

The only information currently available about Manx partnerships in Guinea vessels comes from the Liverpool Trade and Shipping database 1744 to 1786.[16] The Du Bois CD ROM, which will provide a more complete range of information about Guinea vessel ownerships, was not available at the time of going to press. Any additional data that this provides about Manx partnerships in Guinea vessels, not only belonging to Liverpool but also to other ports, will be incorporated in the Manx Merchant Directory – see The Next Stage section in the Conclusion.

Any partnership had to be set up before the vessel could obtain her Plantation Register for the Guinea voyage. There were as many different ownership patterns as there were owners: 'It was possible to be a partner with one person for a venture or two, and to be partners with different individuals or groups at the same time in different ventures'.[94] These patterns are illustrated in Table 7.1 and Appendix 4.

The Liverpool Trade and Shipping database covers two significant periods of the Isle of Man's involvement in the Atlantic slave trade. Some of the data slightly predates 1744 so that information is available on vessel partnerships from the early 1740s until 1765 i.e. the main period when the Guinea goods were being imported into the Island. The database then continues to 1786 [apart from a gap in new registrations of vessels between 1774 and 1778]. This coincides with the first twenty years of the post Revestment period.

At first the Manx merchants appear to have concentrated on the cargo-supply side of the Guinea trade. The earliest Liverpool partnership found was that of Abraham Vianna in a vessel called the *Vianna* in 1757. An application for his naturalisation had been presented to the Duke of Atholl by Crosbies & Trafford of Liverpool.[111] When it was suggested that a Manx-based agent of the then London firm of Da Costa, Vianna & Osorio could be used as their Island contact, the Liverpool merchants were adamant – it had to be Vianna. He was naturalised and, either as an individual or in partnership, he imported Guinea goods valued at over £2,000. The *Vianna* made one Guinea voyage. The Crosbies & Trafford were not partners – see Appendix 4.

The majority of Manx merchants only became interested in vessel partnerships in the period immediately before Revestment – the *Prince Vada* was registered in 1760. Their interest expanded after Revestment – ten of John Joseph Bacon's fourteen Guinea voyages were after 1765 and Paul Bridson owned vessels in 1768 and 1769. In contrast, by 1752 Manx slave captains were becoming owners of the vessels in which they sailed. One of the motives behind this was to ensure that the captain would take as much care as possible during the voyage. Ambrose Lace is one example of a new breed – a captain who left the sea to become a merchant. This meant that he brought to the partnerships his experience of trading actually on the west African coast. His vessel partnerships once he was land-based are listed in Table 7.2. His role in the subsequent success of these partnerships on the west African coast is described in Chapter 9.

Table 7.1: Robert Kennedy's Guinea Vessel Partners[16]

1. Thomas Hodgson, Edward Cropper senior & junior, Charles Cooke and Robert Jennings:
   Molly   (2 voyages)
   Warree   (2 voyages)

2. Charles Cooke, Edward Cropper, Robert Jennings, Robert Clay & John Davies:
   Nancy (1 voyage) and after rebuilding (1 voyage) without Robert Clay as a partner.
   On both occasions John Davies was captain.

3. Charles Cooke only as co-owner:
   Favourite (2 voyages)
   Lord Cassils (1 voyage)

4. William Earle, John Maddrell, Robert Jennings, Michael Finch and John Davies (captain):
   Ann (1 voyage)

5. William Earle & John Tittle:
   Lord Cassills (1 voyage)

6. John Maddrell, George Clowes, John Davies and John Kennedy (captain):
   Ann (2 voyages)

7. Himself, sole owner:
   Carrick (2 voyages)

8. Patrick Black, John Clowes and Wingfield Harding:
   Lord Cassils (2 voyages)

9. Patrick Black, John Parker and John Clowes:
   May (1 voyage)

10. Hugh Pringle:
    Industry (1 voyage)
    Carrick (1 voyage); *Robert* (1 voyage)

11. John Parker and William Davenport:
    May (2 voyages)

12. James Clemens and William Davenport:
    Thomas (1 voyage)

A wide range of information is included in Appendix 4. There are details of the vessels, their crews and the number of slaves that they planned to carry from west Africa to the West Indies or America.

No vessels have been illustrated in this book. One reason is that there was a wide variation within each vessel type. This is indicated in the tonnages quoted in Appendix 4: a ship could be anything from 80 to 200 tons. Frequently vessels were rebuilt between voyages – and their type changed. Readers particularly interested in what the Guinea vessels looked like are referred to the article by Minchinton.[112]

Partnerships

There were three patterns of partnership in a Guinea vessel:

❖ A group of merchants would combine together to form a 'venture'. Their motives would be expanding trade – they may have been in the Guinea trade already – either as a supplier of goods or with experience from previous partnerships. Some of these became very successful, and wealthy men. Those without any experience in the trade often only participated in a partnership for one voyage.

❖ Sometimes the captain of the vessel would be one of the partners. Some captains continued in this role for several years. Others would only be a partner for one voyage – there could be innumerable reasons why he did not join a partnership with the same owners for a second venture.

❖ At a later stage in their careers some of these captains left the sea and settled in Liverpool, as merchants in their own right. If they continued in the Guinea trade then they would be a valuable asset to any partnership.

Manx Merchants

Between 1744 and 1786 nine Manx merchants were co-partners in Liverpool Guinea vessels (see Appendix 4a). Six of these merchants were born and bred on the Isle of Man. Robert Kennedy, Robert Gordon and Abraham Vianna, as already discussed, were naturalised. They had all imported Guinea goods into the Island.

Robert Kennedy was the chief Manx co-owner of Liverpool Guinea vessels during the period studied. He arrived on the Isle of Man as Governor Murray's servant and settled at Castletown, where he subsequently became a merchant. He was naturalised in 1756 and in 1763, together with David Ross, Robert Mercer, Robert Gordon, and other Scottish merchants, he petitioned the Duke of Atholl for permission to introduce a Presbyterian clergyman into the Island.[113]

Kennedy was also one of the principal merchants who signed the letter to the Duke in 1764 about the problems caused by the revenue cutters which had 'lately visited and boarded ships and other vessels in the bays near the shore, and plundered them of such merchandise and effects as they took on board in this Isle'. The purpose of this letter was to forewarn the Duke that unless this external intervention ceased 'your petitioners will be under an absolute necessity of declining all further connections in trade and of withdrawing to some other kingdom or country, where business may be carried on with greater safety and protection'.[114] Other signatories of this petition who were partners in Guinea vessels were: John Joseph Bacon, Hugh Cosnahan, Robert Gordon and Co, James Oates and William Quayle.

By 1764 Kennedy had imported over £13,000 worth of Guinea goods – he is 9th on the list in Table 2.1. As a result he was experienced in the goods required for the trade. He was involved in twelve 'loose partnerships' in Guinea vessels (see Table 7.1). Two of these partners, William Davenport and William Earle, were major Liverpool merchants. Kennedy's sister

Margaret had married into one of the local Castletown families - John Maddrell was co-partner in two of Kennedy's slave vessels. These vessels undertook twenty-four voyages. In some cases the captain was co-owner.

John Joseph Bacon was a partner in five Guinea vessels, which undertook fourteen voyages between 1760 and 1772. Hugh Cosnahan and William Quayle were two of his partners in the *Prince Vada*. James Oates suggested that Phil Moore was also involved in this vessel.[109] If this were really the case, then it illustrates the difficulties of reconstructing partnerships in Guinea vessels.

Davenport mentioned the brig *Prince Vada* in his accounts. John Reily in Dublin had sent 15 tierces of beef costing £37 6s 11d to Liverpool – the duty, freight, entry at the custom house and landwaiter's fee had added a charge of £4 5s 10d. He also mentioned that he had supplied 70 barrels of gunpowder valued at £350 for her cargo. It is not clear whether the gunpowder had been purchased in Liverpool or supplied through Davenport by way of the Island.[115] It is believed that Patrick Black was John Black's son and so brother to Robert Black of Douglas. Patrick had been a Guinea captain before settling in Liverpool as a merchant. Together with Ambrose Lace he remained a favourite with the slave dealers at Old Calabar (see below).

William Snell of London was one of Bacon's regular co-owners and a partner in the *Rumbold*, registered in 1764. A merchant banker in London, Snell had several links with the Island – he had been George Moore's correspondent before a misunderstanding over the insurance of a vessel in the West Indian rum trade.

Michael Finch captained two of Bacon's vessels: the *Rumbold I* and the *Rumbold II*. When he left the sea he stayed in Liverpool where he was partner in five Guinea vessels – two of these, the *Hare* and the *Venus*, with Bacon.

Hugh Cosnahan was involved with James Oates in the *Douglas*, Michael Finch captain, which sailed from Liverpool with the *Marquis of Granby*, Ambrose Lace, in 1762. She called at the Island on her way to the Guinea coast (see Chapter 2 and Appendix 2.5b).

There were no other recognisably Manx partners in Paul Bridson's two vessels. Neither was he co-partnered with his son-in-law, William Boats, in any of Boats's many ventures during this period. It is unclear whether or not the John Johnson listed as a co-owner of the *Bridson* was also a merchant banker in London. This John Johnson was involved with John Callin, John Kelly and Robert Arthur in tea ventures from Gothenburg. He appears throughout the court records as owed sums of money by other Manx merchants. There is no evidence of a direct link with Bridson but this would seem to have been likely. Bridson's death in 1772 [remembering that he was then 78 years old] prevented any further partnerships in Guinea vessels.

In September 1768 Robert Arthur instructed James Montgomerie, captain of the *Kennedy*, that after unloading his cargo of rum at Dunkirk he was to 'proceed to Liverpool to sell the schooner ... There is not the smallest chance of selling her at Greenock. Everybody here thinks Liverpool the only place where there's any chance of selling her, as she is fit for the Guinea trade'[116] Also in 1768 a partnership was formed between John Callin, Hugh Connor, Lewis Geneste, John Geneste and John Rowe of Boston in the schooner *Dolphin*. This vessel does not appear to have been the Kennedy – she had been built at Georgetown, Massachusetts. Although she was prepared for the African trade, the vessel was sold to a partnership which included Miles Barber. The name was changed to the *Francis*.

Table 7.2: Ambrose Lace's Guinea partnerships in Liverpool

Date	Name of Vessel	Voyages	Captains
1758	*Marlborough*	2	William Benson, Matthew Jones
1760	*Eadith*	2	Thomas Jordan
1763	*Betty*	1	Roger Williams, David Evans, Thomas Wane
1765	*Dalrymple*	4	James Berry, Alexander Allason, Patrick Fairweather
1765	*Phoenix*		John Washington, Thomas Seaman
1765	*Young Tom*	1	Henry Stanley
1766	*Polly*	1	John Powr
1767	*Little Britain*	3	Henry Madden, Powell, John Powr
1768	*Ann*	3	James Draper, Duncan McVicar, John Powr, David Brown
1768	*Patty*	5	Robert Parkinson, John Forsythe
1769	*Andromache*	2	James Sharp
1770	*Swift*	1	John Sime
1770	*Shark*	1	Duncan McVicar
1771	*Swift*	5	William Seaton, James Sharp, William Brigstock, William Brighouse
1772	*Dreadnought*	3	John Copper
1773	*Andromache*	1	James Benn Rowe, Edward Dugan
1773	*Dalrymple*	2	Patrick Fairweather
1773	*King George*	1	James Sharpe, James Grundy
1781	*Liverpool Hero*	3	John Copper, John Savage
1783	*Quixote*	3	John Bailllie, Thomas Cooper

59

Several of Ambrose Lace's partnerships were with William Davenport and the vessels appear in the Davenport accounts.[117] The detailed figures are not quoted here as it is not known what share Lace held in any vessel and therefore what fraction of the profit/loss of an individual voyage would have been paid to him. Other partners included Edward Chaffers (see Chapter 9). The increase in numbers of vessels/voyages from one vessel in 1758 to several during the 1770s suggests an increase in Lace's prosperity. Only one Manx captain was employed on these vessels: Edward Dugan.

A letter quoted in Gomer Williams emphasises the importance of getting the structure of a partnership, and the captain of the vessel, right. These are some of the comments made by Grandy King George of Old Town, Old Calabar in a letter dated 13 January 1773. The spelling has been modernised but no attempt has been made to alter the phraseology – the meaning is sufficiently clear. 'So my friend marchant Lace if you send ship to my water again send good man all same yourself and same marchant Black [Patrick Black]. No send old man or man want to be grandy man, if he want to be grandy man let him stand home for marchant one time, no let him come here or all same Captain [James] Sharp. He very good man'. He was also impressed by Sharpe's second mate: 'A young man and a very good man. He is much liked by me and all my people of Calabar, so if you please to send him [as captain of a ship] he will make as quick a dispatch as any man you can send'.[8]

Letters of Instruction
Once the captain of the vessel had been appointed, it was essential for the partners to give him a letter of instruction. These letters provide intimate details of the possible problems that might face the captains on the Guinea voyage. At least five letters have survived for captains with Manx connections: John Murray and Thomas Brownbell of the *Blessing* (1700), Ambrose Lace of the *Marquis of Granby* (1762), Ambrose Lace to William Benson of the *Marlborough* (1770), Charles Kneal of the *Lottery* (1802) and Caesar Lawson of the *Enterprze* (1803).

In July 1801 Hugh Crow was about to set sail on his fourth voyage as captain of the Aspinall vessel the *Will*. 'On the eve of our departure I looked at my instructions, which had, on former occasions, been, as the Americans would say, "considerable lengthy", and to my surprise they were nearly in effect as brief and pointed as: Crow! Mind your eye!'[4] This refers to the fact that Hugh Crow had lost an eye during his childhood, but his owner, Mr Aspinall, reckoned that the other eye was 'a piercer'.

Crow's experience on this occasion was not typical, as can be seen from the three full letters to Manx captains that have survived. Gomer Williams quotes Ambrose Lace's instructions dated 14 April 1762 as captain of the *Marquis of Granby*.[34] The instructions in this letter are so detailed that one might think it was Lace's first voyage as an African captain: 'You are now ready to sail for Africa, America, and back to Liverpool. The cargo we have shipped on board is consigned to you for sale ... and we give you these our orders to be observed in the course of your intended voyage'. In fact it was his sixth Guinea voyage but the first one for these owners, who included William Boats.

Usually the captain would be expected to read the instructions in front of one or more of his owners and sign a document confirming his acceptance of them. This is Charles Kneal's statement: 'I acknowledge to have received form Messrs Thomas Leyland & Co the orders of which the aforegoing is a true copy and I engage to execute them as well as their further orders, the dangers of the sea excepted, as witness my hand this 21st May 1802'.[10]

Additional instructions would be sent to the captains to meet them at all their ports of call, particularly in the Americas. Kneal was instructed: 'On your arrival there [Barbados] call on Messrs Barton Higginson & Co with whom you will find our further orders to govern you in prosecuting the remainder of the voyage. In running down for that Island great care must be taken not to miss it because the want of our instructions would probably be the ruin of the adventure ... you must write to us by every opportunity with a copy of your preceding letter that we may not experience the anxiety and vexation which is always the consequence when the master neglects to perform that part of his duty'.[10]

Figure 8.1 Captain Hugh Crow (1765-1829)

8

The Triangular Voyage

[signature: Hugh Crow]

Table 8.1: Hugh Crow's Guinea Voyages

Date	Vessel	Position	Date	Vessel	Position
1790	*Prince*	Chief Mate	1799	*Will*	Captain
1791	*Bell*	Mate	1800	*Will*	Captain
1792	*Jane*	Second Mate	1801	*Will*	Captain
1794	*Gregson*	Chief Mate	1802	*Ceres*	Captain
1795	*Anne*	Chief Mate	1806	*Mary*	Captain
1796	*James*	Mate	1807	*Kitty's Amelia*	Captain
1798	*Will*	Captain			

When Hugh Crow died in 1829 he left £200 to his executors with the instructions that it should be applied towards 'the expenses attending the preparing for printing and publication a sketch of my life'. This caused the executors some embarrassment in the post-abolitionist era. After a semi-apologetic introduction to *The Memoirs of the Late Captain Hugh Crow* they concluded 'how far soever he may have been mistaken in his opinions, his conduct through life was uniformly regulated by an undeviating adherence to integrity, and an uniform regard to the dictates of humanity'.[4] The *Memoirs* are one of the most frequently quoted contemporary records of the slave trade. They also provide an excellent story, which has stood the test of time. In the present context they have been used to provide the broad outline of the so-called triangular voyage:

Outward from Britain to Africa

Across the Atlantic from Africa to the 'Americas' – the Middle Passage

Homeward from the Americas to England, Scotland etc

The Outward Voyage

Before Revestment, the Isle of Man's central location in the Irish Sea meant that it was possible for vessels calling there to use either route round Ireland. George Moore's attempts to develop Peel harbour were because it was 'extremely convenient to the North Channel through which is found a convenient passage in time of war to America and Africa for the Liverpool ships, the Lancaster and Whitehaven ships'.[79]

At other times the South Channel was favoured as a more direct route to Africa. The *Douglas* and *Marquis of Granby*, both of which had called at Douglas, used the southern route in 1762.[34] In 1801 the *Will*, Hugh Crow, sailing directly from Liverpool, was involved in an incident with a naval flotilla in the South Channel as a result of which several of his crew were impressed (see Chapter 10).

The temperamental weather in the Irish Sea caused a major problem for the Guinea traders. There is some evidence that the Liverpool merchants attempted to avoid the potentially worst weather by clearing out as few vessels as possible during the stormy season. As Christopher Hasell wrote to his gunpowder suppliers in London, 'No more vessels will clear out this season'. There could be other reasons for this pattern. Hasell commented in a letter dated 26 December 1766 'We have very few ships fitting out. The Guinea trade has been so exceedingly bad'.[118] Considering the date, possibly Revestment was one of the reasons for these problems.

In April 1769 the *Rumbold*, Michael Finch captain, put into Ramsey Bay, damaged.[16] Appendix 2 lists Guinea vessels actually wrecked on the Isle of Man or ashore there. The case of Thomas Dickson of the *Charming Nancy* returning part of his Guinea cargo to the Island was described in Chapter 2.

Having left the Irish Sea, the outward voyage took the slaving vessels past the coasts of Europe and North Africa to the Guinea coast. It was highly likely that they would see several enemy vessels during this voyage, even if they did not have an actual encounter with one. Both John Newton's journal of the voyage of the *Duke of Argyle* in 1750 and the remarks on the voyage of the *Ranger*, John Corran captain, in 1789 include details of every vessel observed at sea, and a comment about her nationality. For example, at 9 a.m. on 13 September 1750 the *Duke of Argyle* saw a large ship to the southward and got to the windward of her 'being apprehensive of the Barbary cruisers'. She was a French vessel.[119]

Ambrose Lace's instructions said: 'should you be fortunate enough to take any vessel or vessels from the enemy we recommend your sending them home or to Cork, whichever will be most convenient so as not to distress your own ship'.[34] Thomas Leyland & Co informed Caesar Lawson of the *Enterprize* that they had taken out letters of marque for the vessel [a commission granted by the admiralty to a merchant ship to cruise against and make prizes of the enemy's ships].[18] Any vessel that he captured was to be sent back to Liverpool 'under the care of an active Prize master'. As they approached the port, the Prize Master was to 'hoist a white flag at the fore and one at the main top gallant mast-heads' so confirming that he was not an enemy vessel. This would be answered 'by a signal at the light house'.[120]

Lawson sailed from Liverpool on 20 July 1803. On 26 August he 'detained' the Spanish brig *St Augustin*, Josef Anto de Ytuno captain, on her voyage from Malaga to Vera Cruz. She was sent back to England and arrived at Hoylake on 25 October. There were two problems. Lawson's letter of marque did not include Spanish vessels and Britain was not at war with Spain. Damages had to be paid to her owners by Thomas Leyland & Co, so reducing rather than increasing the profits of the voyage.[120]

Figure 8.2: The Outward Voyage

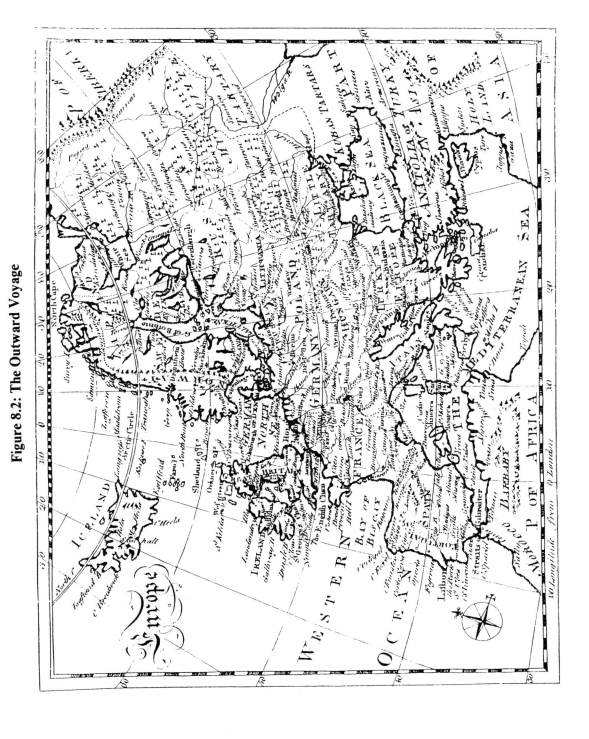

There was the alternative possibility – that the British Guinea ship might be captured by a vessel from a hostile nation. Ambrose Lace was told that as both the *Marquis of Granby* and the *Douglas* were ships of force, 'we hope tolerably well manned, you will be better able to defend yourselves against the enemy. We therefore recommend your keeping a good look out that you may be prepared against an attack'.[34] Neither of these captains was ever involved in encounters with the enemy on any of their voyages.

Other vessels were not so fortunate (see Chapter 12). There is some evidence of Manxmen in French gaols, though how they arrived there is unclear. Daniel Kneale of Lezayre died on 28 February 1779 in a gaol at Angiers [Angers]. John Christory of Douglas died in the same gaol the following March. He and William Quirk had both been in prison at Fenigiers[?] before they were transferred to Angiers. Nothing is known of the fate of William Quirk after he gave evidence back on the Island in July 1781. Nor is it known whether he was released from the prison in France, or escaped as Hugh Crow did (see Chapter 12). James Irving, captain of the *Anna*, appears to have sailed too close the North African coast – and was shipwrecked. Several of the crew, including the first mate, John Clague [Clegg], were 'taken prisoner by Algerine pirates and kept as a slave'.[121]

The length of the passage from Liverpool to West Africa could vary from 'five weeks and a day' to several months. In 1750 John Newton's *Duke of Argyle* took just over eight weeks to reach Sierra Leone. He wrote to his wife: 'The passage from England has not been the shortest, but remarkably pleasant, and free from disaster'.[119] The *Will*, Hugh Crow, sailed from Liverpool with the *Lord Stanley* in October 1800. They encountered 'some severe gales of wind' during a ten-week passage.[4] The *Anne*, Reuben Wright captain and Hugh Crow chief mate, sailed from Liverpool in 1795 with the *Old Dick* and the *Eliza*, 'but soon after parted company in a gale of wind'. The *Anne* was becalmed off the Cape de Verde islands for about a month during which time the crew 'suffered much for want of water'. When she reached Bonny 'to our astonishment, we saw the two ships we had parted with, come to anchor about a quarter of an hour before us. We thus all arrived as nearly at the same moment, after being separated, at sea, for upwards of fourteen weeks'.[4]

At the Guinea coast
There were several problems on the Guinea coast, apart from the necessity of obtaining a cargo of slaves as quickly as possible. The coast itself was dangerous – there were sudden hurricanes, sandy bars crossed the river mouths so that there was insufficient water for the ships' boats, let alone the vessels themselves to cross safely and the climate was not conducive to good health on the part of the crews. These points will be expanded in Chapters 10 to 12.

Trading Problems
The trade on the coast could be disrupted by friction between the vessels trading there, by too few slaves on the coast, possibly because of local wars, or by other local problems, such as the death of the king. Hugh Crow's first voyage to Africa was as chief mate of the *Prince*. Having left Liverpool in October 1790, they arrived at Anamaboe on the Gold Coast in December. 'We lay there about three weeks without transacting any trade, the king of that part of the coast having died some time before, in consequence of which all business was suspended'.[4]

Crow was to suffer from an even greater delay. The *Jane*, Reuben Wright, sailed from Liverpool in June 1792. 'Just on our arrival old King Pepple died. Three months elapsed before the chiefs and priests agreed on whom they should appoint as regent until the son of the deceased came of age'.[4]

There was seldom only one vessel trading on the coast at any particular time. As Leyland & Co wrote to Charles Kneal of the *Lottery*, who was going to Bonny: 'You will most certainly have to contend with five or six vessels but we trust the masters will study the interest of their owners and unite with you in every effort to keep down the prices'. At the same time Kneal was not to compete with Caesar Lawson of the *Louisa*. Instead 'you are mutually to assist each other with goods and boats to forward the trade of both ships and you are not on any account to oppose each other in any way that will operate to our prejudice'. Another Leyland vessel, the *Enterprize*, captain Egerton, would be at Old Calabar. If he needed assistance then Kneal was to provide this only 'without prejudice to your own voyage'.[10]

On his arrival at Old Calabar Ambrose Lace was instructed 'if one or more ships be there, you will observe to make an agreement with the master or masters so as not to advance the price of the slaves on each other'.[34] Lace's experiences during and after the massacre at Old Calabar are described in Chapter 9. This will show that the local traders were not always co-operative. On his last voyage to Africa in 1754, as captain of the *Knight* William Boats was in a dispute with the natives at Anamaboe. In 1771 the *Cato*, William Gill captain, was 'cut-off' in the Ben river and all the crew were killed.

Before leaving the African coast the vessel took on board sufficient supplies for both the slaves and the crew on the Middle Passage. Kneal was instructed that when he had obtained his slaves and 'laid in a sufficient quantity of yams, wood and water for the middle passage', he was to 'proceed with a press of sail for Barbados'.[10]

The provisions were not always obtained from the African mainland. The islands of Annabon and St Thomas (see Figure 7.1) were also regular ports of call. Crow described the produce of St Thomas as 'beans called calavancies, plantains, casavi root, and the usual vegetable productions of tropical countries'. While collecting provisions there he had time to take 'a tourist trip to the remains of the bishop's palace with captain Tool of the brig *Ruby* of Liverpool'. When he was ready to sail, the governor, 'with whom I had contracted an intimacy' gave Crow several present 'amongst which were some monkeys'.[4]

The Middle Passage
The captains were instructed to take care of the slaves. As Crow explained 'I took great pains to promote the health and comfort of all on board by proper diet, regularity, exercise, and cleanliness; for I considered that on keeping the ship clean and orderly, which was always my hobby, the success of our voyage mainly depended'.[4]

Kneal was told 'In your treatment of the negroes, show them every indulgence that will be consistent with the safety of the ship; do not suffer your officers or crew to offer the least abuse to them; take care that their provisions are cooked in that way which is most agreeable to them'.[10]

Crow described the food fed to the slaves on the Middle Passage. 'In addition to yams we gave them, for a change, fine shilled beans and rice cooked together, and this was served up to each individual with a plentiful proportion of the soup. On other days their soup was mixed with peeled yams cut up thin and boiled with a proportion of pounded biscuit. For the sick we provided strong soup and middle messes, prepared from mutton, goats'-flesh, fowls etc to which were added sago and lilipees, the whole mixed with port wine and sugar ... A dram of brandy bitters was given to each of the men, and, clean spoons being served out, they breakfasted about nine o'clock ... A middle mess of bread and cocoa-nuts was given them about mid-day. The third meal was served out about three o'clock'.[4]

Figure 8.3: The Middle Passage and the Homeward Voyage

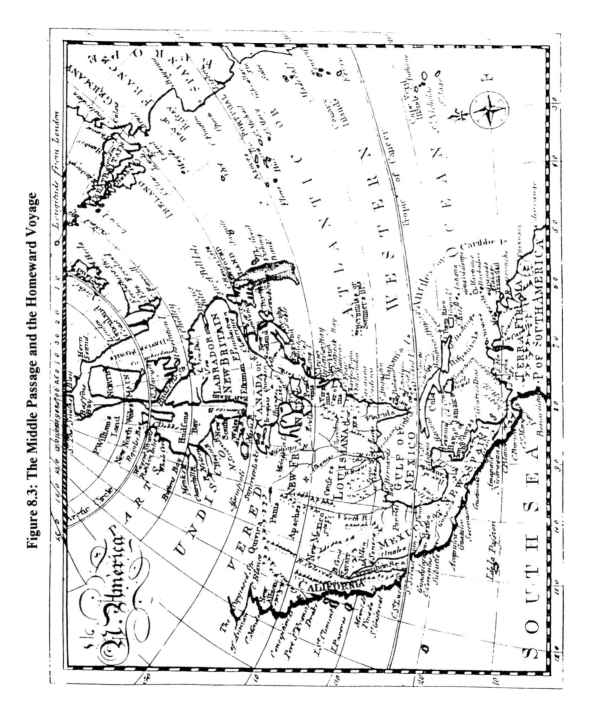

There were other ways to keep the slaves healthy. When the *Will* arrived at Bonny in 1798 'One of our first occupations was the construction of a regular thatched house on the deck, for the accommodation and comfort of the salves. This building extended from stem to stern, and was so contrived that the whole ship was thoroughly aired, while at the same time the blacks were secured from getting overboard. These temporary buildings would cost from £30 to £40, according to the size of the ship'.[4]

Crow described the daily routine. 'Their personal comfort was also carefully studied. On their coming on deck about eight o'clock in the morning, water was provided to wash their hands and faces, a mixture of lime juice to cleanse their mouths, towels to wipe with, and chew sticks to clean their teeth ... About eleven, if the day were fine, they washed their bodies all over'. Once they were dry, they were given an opportunity of amusing themselves (see Chapter 1) before they were allowed to dance or run about in deck 'to keep them in good spirits'.[4] They went down below again at four or five in the evening.

Privateers were a problem once more as the vessels approached the West Indies. One of William Boats's more famous exploits was in 1758. The *Knight* was challenged by a French privateer with 'twelve carriage guns and full of men' just off the Leeward Islands. Boats armed some of his slaves and finally managed to get clear of the other vessel. He landed 360 slaves in Jamaica – out of a total cargo of 398. Caesar Lawson was successful in recapturing the *John* of Liverpool with 261 slaves on board. She was taken to Dominica. The cost of repairing the *John* was also a charge against the voyage. These reduced the overall profit.[120]

The length of the middle passage varied. The *Ranger*, John Corran, sailed from Anamaboe in June and arrived at Kingston harbour 57 days later on 23 August 1790. The exact route taken by the vessel is shown in figure 14.1. The distance covered was 5,385 miles at an average rate of 94 miles per day. This varied considerably from less than 50 miles while still close to the African coast to over 150 miles nearer the West Indies.[122] 'We arrived there [Kingston, Jamaica] after a toilsome passage from St Thomas of about eight weeks'.[4]

The West Indies
The market for the slaves in the West Indies depended on where they had been purchased in Africa. Brownbell and Murray of the *Blessing* were told that if the slaves had been obtained from the Gold Coast or Whydah the ship was to 'touch at' Barbados 'where if you find the markets reasonable good sell there'. If the markets were dull then they were to sail to the leeward 'to which island you shall see convenient, where dispose of your negroes to our best advantage'. The money obtained from selling the slaves was to be invested in sugar, cottons and ginger 'if to be had' and the *Blessing* was to return home as soon as possible. It was anticipated that the money would purchase more goods than she could carry home. In that case the balance was to left in the hands of some 'honest man' to be sent on freight to either London or Liverpool.

If, however, the slaves had come from Angola, they were to head for where the contact was Mr Holsted, and the vessel loaded with sugar, cotton, ginger and indigo. Mr Murray and the doctor were to be sent down to Carthagena with some of the slaves, which were to be sold for 'weighty' pieces of eight.[19]

If Ambrose Lace sold his slaves at Guadeloupe or Martinico or the Leeward Islands he was to load the *Marquis of Granby* on the ground tier with 100 casks of good muscado sugar, on the other tiers with white sugar and between decks with cotton and coffee. Any money remaining was to be converted into 'good bills of exchange at as short dates as you can'. If he could not obtain the right price for the slaves there then he was to try Jamaica. Here he was to fill the hold with the very best muscado sugar and ginger, between the decks with cotton, pimento and ten puncheons of rum and for dunnage he was to use broad sound mahogany. Once more the balance was to be in bills of exchange.[34]

There is some evidence of Manxmen living in the West Indies and owning slaves. Charles Moore of Kingston, Surrey, Jamaica, who described himself as master mariner, made his will in 1801. He left to his father, John Moore of Derbyhaven, all his real estate in Isle of Man and interest on £1,000 to be invested in public funds in Great Britain. Then he left Ann Hindes of Kingston, a free woman of colour, £500 British and the rest of his estate, after the following bequests: Eleanor Elizabeth Clark and William James Clark, the free children of colour of Mary Hindes, £100 each to buy mourning; Eleanor Elizabeth Mun, a free back girl, £50 currency of Jamaica; Mary Ann Glegg, daughter of John Glegg mariner, £100 current money; Mrs Elizabeth Glegg a gold mourning ring; Joseph Dennison of Kingston a suit of mourning and each of executors a gold mourning ring. He also stated that 'I do hereby emance and make free my negro man slave named Charles, but generally by the name of Money'. Charles was to have an annual sum of £5 currency of Jamaica during natural life 'as and for the annuity made payable by law to persons manermized'. The will was proved at Kirk Patrick in August 1803.

Although Robert Ferguson was not Manx he died on a Manx vessel and his will was proved on the Island. Originally from Green Hill near Whitehaven, Ferguson went abroad 'several years ago and settled in St Croix where by his honest industry he procured a considerable fortune' as a shoe manufacturer. When he became ill 'desirous to return to his native country for the recovery of his health' on 28 June 1767 he boarded the brigantine *Wolf* of Douglas, William Charles master. Ferguson made his will at sea in presence of William Welch, Thomas Smith, Thomas Young and William Charles. According to this will, he left both to the Danish church and the Hospital in St Croix 10 pieces of 8. Susanne Page (presumably of St Croix) was to inherit all his household furniture and 'a negro wench by the name of Rose'. Finally his brother was to have the remaining four negroes, Betty and her 3 children, with all Ferguson's houses and lands. John Ferguson turned to Peter John Heywood of the Nunnery to explain to the court that he was a collier of Whitehaven 'in the service of Sir James Lowther' with little need for land in the West Indies, let alone Betty et al.

The Homeward Voyage
The homeward passage provided as many hazards as the other sections of the journey. By this time the crew was probably greatly reduced, several of those who sailed from England having died, been paid off in the Americas or been impressed. If the men had been on board since leaving home then they were probably exhausted (see Chapter 12).

In 1798 the *Will*, Hugh Crow, sailed with the fleet 'from which we parted in a gale of wind; but ours was nevertheless the first ship that arrived at Liverpool'.[4] She sailed in convoy again in 1801, leaving Port Royal under the protection of the *York*, a 64-gun vessel under Commodore John Ferriere. 'We remained in Port Antonio three days to collect the homeward bound vessels that were to rendezvous there; and we finally sailed with a fleet of one hundred and sixty-four ships, which, when all under sail, presented a most beautiful appearance. We had a fine passage, and in two days after parting with those of the fleet that were bound to St George's Channel we reached Liverpool '.[4]

Crow's *Ceres* sailed from Dominica for Liverpool in December 1804. Two days later they were 'overtaken by a dreadful gale of wind from the west-north-west; and it continued to

Figure 8.4: The *Ceres*, December 1804

Extract from the 107th Psalm

23 They that go down to the sea in ships : and occupy their business in great waters;

24 These men see the works of the Lord : and his wonders in the deep.

25 For at his word the stormy wind ariseth : which lifteth up the waves thereof.

26 They are carried up to the heaven, and down again to the deep : their soul melteth away because of the trouble

27 They reel to and for, and stagger like a drunken man : and are at their wits' end.

28 So when they cry unto the Lord in their trouble : he delivereth them out of their distress.

29 For he maketh the storm to cease : so that the waves thereof are still.

30 Then are they glad, because they are at rest : and so he bringeth them unto heaven where they would be.[123]

blow gale after gale for ten or twelve days successively. The sea ran mountains high and we were often obliged to lay to, lest the ship should be pooped ... a sea struck us on the larboard quarter, which broke up the mizzen channel bend against the ship's side, and carried away all the iron stanchions on the larboard gangway. A part of this tremendous wave went as high as the maintop, which it literally dashed in pieces and carried away. Our main-topmast went overboard with a crash, and the ship's waist being deep, and holding much water, one poor fellow was washed away and perished, and several others were with difficulty saved. Another sea carried away our quarter deck rails and bulwarks, and a fine Newfoundland dog was washed overboard. How we escaped foundering God only knows, for, at one time, our main deck was breast high with water, under the weight of which the ship staggered, with scarcely any power of buoyancy. Some of the guns also broke loose, and, before they could be secured, were dashed from side to side and did a great deal of damage. A quantity of water likewise got below and did considerable injury to the cargo [sugar and coffee] ... Our situation during the gale was at one time so perilous, when the sea broke wildly over the decks and though the rigging, that we could not look back upon it without thinking of "The sweet little Cherub that sits up aloft, looking out for the life of poor Jack." In the height of our distress I often called to mind the 107th psalm, which so beautifully expresses the feelings by which we were impressed in the hour of danger (see Figure 8.3)'.[4]

Hugh Crow continued to command vessels to the end of the slave trade. The *Kitty's Amelia* was one of the last to clear from Liverpool in July 1807. He then purchased property on the Isle of Man and spent the next few years commuting between the Island and Liverpool. The next chapter describes Ambrose Lace's experiences at Africa.

9

On the African Coast

Amb.e Lace

The idea that a Guinea vessel arrived at the African coast, started to trade, took the slaves on board and set off again within a short period of time is very far from the truth. The slaves could only be purchased according to the local custom and the captain would have to be prepared to negotiate with the traders accordingly. Each owner tended to trade on one particular part of the coast. This meant that the captains could develop a rapport with the locals: Hugh Crow with King Pepple and Ambrose Lace with the chiefs of Old Town, Old Calabar. Between 1785 and 1795 Boats sent two-thirds of his slave voyages to Bonny and Jamaica.[124]

The letters of instruction would be specific about the types of slaves that were to be purchased. Lace's cargo of goods was intended to be sufficient to purchase 550 slaves. He must 'mind to be very choice' in his selection and to 'buy no distempered or old ones'.[34] Lawson's negroes should be strong while Kneal was to receive only those that were 'well-made, full chested, vigorous and without bodily imperfection'.[10] Newton rejected some of the slaves that he was offered – they were too small or ill-formed. One of the reasons for this care in the choice of the slaves was so that they would 'stand' or 'bear' the passage to the West Indies, reducing the mortality rate and ensuring a profit on the voyage. Another reason was that they should be suitable for their market. Newton mentions exchanging some small girl slaves with an American ship which was on the coast for a cargo of children.

There were also instructions about the sex of the slaves. Kneal's cargo of 290 was to consist of half 'prime men negroes' from 15 to 25 years old; 3/8 boys from 10 to 15 and 1/8 women from 10 to 18. Lawson was requested that his cargo be all males 'if possible to get them. At any rate buy as few females as in your power, because we look to a Spanish market for the disposal of your cargo, where females are a very tedious sale. In the choice of the negroes be very particular ... and do not buy any above 24 years of age, as it may happen that you will have to go to Jamaica, where you know any exceeding that age would be liable to a duty of £10 per head'.[120] Additional goods were often purchased in Africa, either for sale in the Americas or to be brought home. Lace should have £400 to spare after purchasing his slaves which he was to 'lay out in ivory, which we recommend your purchasing from the beginning of your trade'. Kneal's cargo of palm oil was described in Chapter 1.

The following chapters are based on the experiences of Manx slave traders in different parts of the Guinea coast. John Bridson was the chief mate on board the *Duke of Argyle*, John Newton captain on her 1750 voyage to Sierra Leone (see Chapter 10). John Corran was captain of the *Ranger* when she went to the Gold Coast in 1790 and Table 9.1 tabulates her first few weeks on the coast. Other aspects of this voyage are described in Chapter 11. When the *William*, Richard Hart captain, sailed to the Congo river in 1800, Charles Christian was the surgeon on board. Chapter 12 includes some of the events which happened on this voyage. Ambrose Lace was captain of the *Edgar*, which was at Old Calabar in 1762.

11 January 1790	Cape Lahoe	At 9 a.m. got a canoe from the shore
13 January 1790	Pickeny Bassam	At 4 p.m. canoe
14 January 1790	Grand Bassam	At 6 a.m. 5 canoes came off from but no trade
16 January 1790	Assignee	7 a.m. came off some natives and made trade for some rolls of tobacco. At 11 a.m. the natives left us. Sent 20 rolls on board the long boat and sent her in shore
17 January 1790	Appalonia Fort	Came off some of the natives. Sold 3 rolls tobacco.
18 January 1790	Appalonia Fort	Sold 15 rolls tobacco.
19 January 1790	Appalonia Fort	No canoes came off
23 January 1790	Annamaboe Fort	Employed in taking some goods off from the Fort
24 January 1790	Annamaboe Fort	Remainder of goods from Fort
25 January 1790	Annamaboe Fort	Employed in taking some of the guns from the shore
26 January 1790	Annamaboe Fort	6 a.m. sent schooner boat [the *Betsey*?] to Cape Coast to barter with an American for rum … at meridian boat returned without rum
27 January 1790	Annamaboe Fort	2 p..m. Captain Corran went on board an American in the roads and made a barter for some rum. Employed in sending goods on board schooner *Betsey*. (No trade)
28 January 1790	Annamaboe Fort	8 p.m. schooner to Windward Coast
29 January 1790	Annamaboe Fort	Sent *Gregson* pinnace up to Cape Coast for water
26 March 1790	Annamaboe Fort	Heavy swell occasioning such a surf impossible for the natives to come off.
14 April 1790	Annamaboe Fort	Goods on board schooner boat and 4 weeks food.
17/18 April 1790	Annamaboe Fort	Traded for gold
22 April 1790	Pickeny Bassam	
25 April 1790	Pickeny Bassam	Traded for gold.

Source: Remarks on the voyage of the *Ranger*[122]

Ambrose Lace appears frequently in the records. He was on board a Guinea vessel at Old Calabar in 1748. By 1751 he was chief mate of the *Neptune*, when William Davenport sold him a cask of gunflints costing £1 1s.[125] He was captain of the *Duke of Chester* on her Guinea voyage in 1754 (see Table 9.1). His letter of instructions as captain of the *Marquis of Granby* have been quoted frequently in the preceding chapters. But by far his most famous exploit was at the massacre of Old Calabar in 1767, when he was in command of the *Edgar*. Shortly after this he left the sea and became a successful merchant in Liverpool. He died in 1794.

Old Town and New Town were on opposite sides of the Cross River, which flows into the Bight of Biafra, immediately east of the Niger delta (see Figure 9.1). When Lace was there in 1748 'there was no inhabitants in the place called Old Town. They all lived at the place called New Town. Some time after, disputes arose between a party, who now called themselves Old Town people, and those who are now called New Town people'. As a result of this dispute 'through fear of each other, for a considerable time, no canoe would leave the towns to go up the river for slaves'.[126]

In 1767 there were nine ships in the Cross River, waiting for their cargoes. These included the *Canterbury*, Captain Sparks from London, the *Duke of York*, James Bivins, the *Indian Queen*, William Floyd and the *Nancy*, James Maxwell from Bristol[127] and the *Edgar*, Ambrose Lace from Liverpool. Several of the captains decided that the only way to obtain any slaves was to try and resolve the dispute. Sparks suggested that they should invite all the locals on board their vessels 'to reconcile themselves'. He then appears to have made a separate agreement with the New Towners – that they should kill all the Old Towners, who were still on board the vessels at eight o'clock in the morning. In the resultant massacre several hundred of the Old Towners were killed and others were taken away as slaves.

As he was one of the captains there at the time, it was believed that Lace had been guilty of involvement in the massacre. When the Reverend Thomas Clarkson visited Liverpool to obtain information for his book *History of the Abolition of the Abolition of the African Slave Trade* he was invited to breakfast with Captain Chaffers and some of his friends. He was introduced to Lace and began asking questions about the Guinea coast. When Lace mentioned Calabar 'a kind of horror came over me ... It almost instantly occurred to me that he commanded the *Edgar* out of Liverpool when the dreadful massacre there took place. Indeed I seemed to be so confident of it, that, attending more to my feelings than to my reason at this moment, I accused him of being concerned in it. This produced great confusion among us. For he looked incensed at Captain Chaffers, as if he had introduced me to him for this purpose. Captain Chaffers again seemed to be all astonishment that I should have known of this circumstance, and to be vexed that I should have mentioned it in such a manner. I was also in a state of trembling myself. Captain Lace could only say that it was a bad business. But he never defended himself nor those concerned in it. We soon parted, to the great joy of us all'.[128]

At the same time a Parliamentary Committee of Enquiry was taking evidence about the slave trade. They had already heard a graphic account about the bloodiness of the massacre from Thomas Rutter, the boatswain on board Sharp's vessel, the *Canterbury*. Now they received the report from Clarkson about Lace's reaction to his accusation. They summoned Lace to give evidence on 12 March 1790. His version of events suggests that rather than having been involved in the planning of the massacre not only did it take him by surprise, but also he feared for his own life. Parts of his evidence have been quoted in full:

> Do you remember, that in order to make an end of a
> dispute which had for some time subsisted between the

inhabitants of the Old and the New Town, any agreement was made for both parties to meet on shipboard? *Yes ...*

Did any of the parties meet on board in consequence of such agreement; and what passed on that occasion? *The principal people from Old Town came on board my ship, where the duke (the principal man of Old Town) was to have met them; they came on board about half past seven in the morning; at about eight I was going to breakfast with a person who called himself King of Old Town; there were four of the King's large canoes alongside of my ship, where the other canoes were I cannot tell; I was just pouring out some coffee, when I heard a firing; the king called out and said Imo, a brother of his, was firing. I went upon deck along with the King, and my people told me my gunner was killed; immediately the King was for going overboard; I then told him to stay where he was; he told me he would not, he would go in his canoe, which he did; his son who was with him in my ship he left behind, but called to him in his own language to stay with me, which he did; the firing, by what I can recollect, might be for 10 or 15 minutes but I cannot be certain as to the exact time. The canoes were most of them then got astern of my ship within about 300 to 400 yards; I had not time to make observations of the two parties. I wanted to defend myself after I was fired into: I was no further molested, the canoes were all gone.*

... Did you or your people take any share in the affray that then happened? *No more than any gentleman in this room ...*

Did you know by whom your gunner was killed? *It was impossible for me to know; it must have been from some of the canoes at a distance, but from which I cannot tell; but I am of opinion the firing must have come from the New Town people.*

Lace said he had brought the King of Old Town's son, young Ephraim, home with him to Liverpool and 'had him at school near two years, then sent him out [back to Africa], he cost me above sixty pounds and when his father's gone I hope the son will be a good man'.[129]

The Committee of Enquiry wrote to Liverpool for further information about the possible education of negroes in the town. They were informed that there were often between 50 and 70 children in and around Liverpool 'natives of Africa', who had been sent 'to receive the advantage of an European education'. It was believed that they also went to London and Bristol. 'The education of these children here is confined to reading, writing, and a little arithmetic, with as much of religion as persons of their age and situation usually receive from their schoolmasters. The girls, beside the above mentioned common school education, acquire some

Figure 9.1: Bonny and Old Calabar

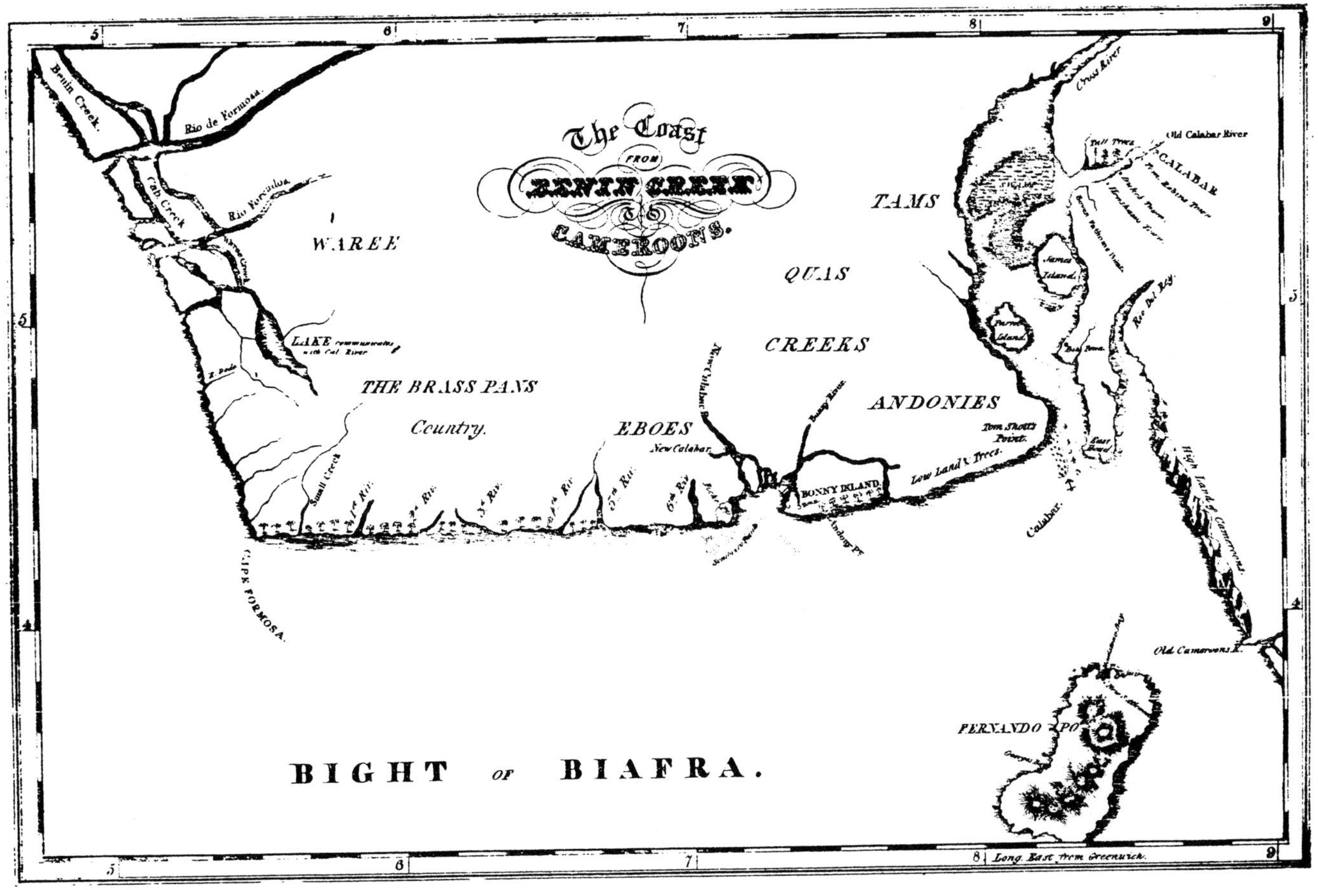

knowledge of domestic duties, and are instructed in needlework. The influence which European education seems to have upon them, after their return to their native country, appears chiefly in their more civilised manner of life. They endeavour to live and dress in European style, to erect their houses in a comfortable and convenient manner, and by a fondness for society, their disposition, we have no doubt, are improved by their education'. The report concluded 'It has always been the practice of merchants and commanders of ships trading to Africa, to encourage the natives to send their children to England, as it not only conciliates their friendship and softens their manners, but adds greatly to the security of the trader, which answers the purposes both of interest and humanity'.[126]

The following letters, which are quoted in Gomer Williams, suggest that Lace remained on good terms with the Old Towners. On 19 July 1773 Robin John Otto Ephraim wrote to Lace: 'I send Joshua one little boy by Captain Cooper ... My mother send your wife one teeth by Captain Sharp ... Send me some writing paper and books my Coomey [custom] is 1600 copper send me two sheep alive. Sir I am your best friend Otto Ephraim'. There were later letters. One from Old Town Calabar, dated 24 December 1775 ended: 'no more at present from your friend, Ephraim Robin John. PS Remember me to your wife'. In August 1776 he reported sending Lace 'one teeth 50 weight' by Cooper and on 20 March 1783 he added in the postscript: 'Remember me to your wife and your sons Joshua, Ambrose, William and Polly'.[130]

The Old Town people had a partial revenge in 1768. Although they were outnumbered ten to one, they succeeded in killing and wounding nearly 300 of the New Towners. George Colley (see Chapter 5), who was now captain of the *Latham* reported 'They seem to be pretty quiet at present. The battle was all in sight, not above a gun shot from the ship, and by that have received the thanks of the New Town people, for not firing at them, as it was Ephraim's particular desire, not to interfere, but to let them fight it out themselves'.[128]

10

Manx Mariners in the Guinea Trade

John Bridson

It is impossible to estimate the total numbers of Manx mariners who sailed on the Guinea vessels from Liverpool, let alone the other British slaving ports. They appear on a high proportion, though not all, of the crew lists and vessel muster rolls that have survived. From the Manx records it has been possible to identify over 300 mariners who died in the Guinea trade between 1700 and 1807. Those who died 'on the Guinea coast' are listed in Appendix 5. Several personal stories have been collected but little is known about the mariners' lives actually on board the Guinea vessels. An exception is the information in John Newton's Journal about John Bridson, the first mate of the *Duke of Argyle* in 1750.

Other Manxmen on board the *Duke of Argyle* were Matthew Curfey [sic] tailor, Edward Lawson and John Corkill, seamen fore-the-mast, and Thomas Bridson, ship's apprentice. On John Newton's *African* voyage in 1753 there was another John Bridson, fore-the-mast. Two of the seamen who signed the crew contract for the *True Blue*, Joshua Hatton captain, on 2 August 1768 were also Manx: Richard Killey and Frederick Kneal.[131] No other contracts signed by Manx mariners were found amongst these documents.

The best non-Manx information about the mariners comes from the Liverpool muster rolls. Some of these had a column labelled 'Place of Abode'. Where these columns are filled in accurately then they include a wide range of places. The *Ceres*, Adam Elliott captain, sailed from Liverpool in April 1804 with a crew of 40 on board.[132] Six of these came from the Isle of Man (see Chapter 12). The others were from:

Liverpool	3	America	6
England	11	Sweden	3
Scotland	1	Gibraltar	1
Ireland	9		

The Crews

The Guinea vessels needed comparatively large crews for their size – to take care of the slaves both on the African coast and during the Middle Passage. Their wages were paid in two parts. There would be a three months' advance – to pay off any debts and support their family while they were at sea – and the balance would be paid on discharge, provided they did not leave the ship without good cause, or mutiny.[131]

Once at the West Indies, the surplus crew members might be discharged, especially if they were sick. Large numbers were also impressed, as the Guinea vessels waiting for their slave sales to be completed were an easy target for the navy. As a result they tended to be brought home by skeletal crews (see Chapter 12).

Crow described some of the crews on board the Guinea vessels. 'Many of the individuals composing them were the very dregs of the community: some of them had escaped from jails; others were undiscovered offenders, who sought to withdraw themselves from their country lest they should fall into the hands of the officers of justice'. He claimed that his crews were different: 'for my own part I was always very lucky to procuring good crews'.[4]

There is an impression that the Manx mariners were of a better calibre than the average crews. One reason for this was that so many of them were 'bred to the sea'. There is also a possibility that after 1765, and the disappearance of ready employment on wherries in the running trade, larger numbers of experienced seamen became available.

John Tear's will was dated 11 October 1769, before he left the Island 'to try my fortune' (see section on the voyage of the *Duke of Argyle*). Charles Wattleworth was only a young 'lad' but as he intended 'speedily to depart this Isle' on 12 May 1760 he made a will. In August he sailed from Liverpool on board the *Charming Fanny*, Michael Finch captain. Having survived the voyage as far as the West Indies, it was believed that he fell overboard on the last night the vessel was at Guadeloupe. The *Charming Fanny* sailed without him. But within a week of her arrival at Liverpool another vessel came in from Guadeloupe. Her crew knew the *Charming Fanny* well, having 'often bought bread and beef from our captain'. They confirmed that a mariner had been found dead in the harbour and the description fitted Wattleworth 'by reason there was no other missed from on board the ship at that time' and because he 'wore his own hair'.

William Kneen was frequently in trouble during the 1730s, apparently for minor misdemeanours.[133] He was beginning to feel persecuted because he was living 'in a country where he is so well known'. In March 1738 he was liable to a trial by jury 'upon the oaths of people who in his own sense did him great injustice'. Whatever the punishment this time, he was convinced that at some stage in the near future 'he may come to a more dreadful fate than the present'. As a result he offered to 'banish himself voluntarily'. This proposal was accepted by Governor Murray, 'although the petitioner is so notorious an offender'. Kneen must enter into a bond of £50 as a security that he would pay his fine and 'depart this Isle within twenty days ... never return to the same again during his life'. If in the future it so happened that he was 'wind driven or put in from sea by stress of weather or such like absolute necessity' then Kneen must 'depart again' either on the same ship or 'by next opportunity'. This would ensure that he was 'no more offensive to the good people of this Isle'.[134] Kneen appears to have gone to Liverpool and entered on board a Guinea vessel. His career lasted for several years as it was not until 1746 that his death was reported to the Consistory Court in the Island. However, as he had not left 'any goods for his children' there was nothing to discuss.

Sometimes the fate of the mariner is not known. In June 1760 Thomas Kneen 'being determined and bound to go a voyage to sea towards the coasts of Africa' made his will. There was no further information received from or about him and so, as it was not certain whether he was 'alive or not', probate was granted on 22 October 1765. Other families waited longer before claiming that their relation was dead. Edmund Quark, a mariner, left the Island in the 1730s. He had not been heard of for over twenty years and so in June 1764 he was presumed dead.

Although there were some horror stories about the treatment of crews in the slave trade, no clear evidence has been found of the abuse of a Manx mariner by his captain. The letters of instruction, however, recommended discipline. Ambrose Lace was told: 'We recommend your keeping good rules and good harmony amongst your crew'[34] while Charles Kneal was encouraged to be 'strict and regular in the discipline on board the ship'.[10]

The Network

The Manx mariners tended to keep together. They witnessed each other's wills and when one died another Manx mariner would frequently make a report about the circumstances to the Consistory Court. They were also well aware of each other's whereabouts. This is particularly clear in letters associated with the death of Daniel Cottiman on board the *Salisbury*, Thomas Marsden captain. When he returned safely to Liverpool in June 1753 [it is not clear whether this had been a Guinea voyage or only from the West Indies] William Cottiman reported to his uncle that he had seen his brother in Jamaica, who would be home in six weeks time 'or thereabouts'. He continued 'Pray give my duty to my stepfather. I am sorry to hear of the death of my mother ... Remember my love to Bridget Cottiman and tell her that her son Daniel Cottiman, cooper, is dead. But the ship will not be at home this four or five months yet'.

Bridget should write either to Daniel Corlett or Philip Cottiman in Liverpool and they would tell her 'what she must do to get his effects'. She contacted both of them. Philip replied on 15 July, confirming that 'There is news from the ship that their cooper is dead, which I am very sorry to hear. But we can do nothing concerning his affairs till the ship comes home. She is at Barbados now'. When the *Salisbury* did return to Liverpool Cottiman would let her know 'and then you may do as you think proper - to come over or no'.

Both Daniel Corlett and Mathew Curphy replied on 24 July 'we were acquainted by the captain and mates letters that he is dead, which doubtless is true. But I do not hear that there is West India news from the ship yet therefore we do not expect her home this three or four months yet'. There is no obvious reason why these two people should have sen these letters. Two of the partners in the vessel, however, were Richard Gildart and Robert Armitage (see Chapter 1).

Before Daniel Cottiman had sailed on the *Salisbury* in August 1752, John Cottier, now of Ramsey, had taken a memorandum [inventory] of his effects left behind in Liverpool. The list included: 'with Mr Joseph Newhouse £45 British at interest per annum; left in the care of Phillip Cottiman tailor: one silver watch No. 609, John Tazah maker, two pair of white cotton stockings, two cravats, two stocks, a silver stock buckle, a blue coat, a black waistcoat and one hat and case, all worth ten shillings, and in cash twelve shillings sterling money. Two linen shirts'. There was also about ten pounds in the hands of a ship doctor 'whose name he had forgot'.

Impressment

The Guinea voyages suffered from the number of wars in which England was involved during the Atlantic slave trade period (see Table 10.1). One problem was the impressment of seamen 'under plea of state necessity - to serve in our men-of-war'.[18] In theory, the solution was to carry a document called a 'protection' - in 1756 four Davenport vessels sailed from Liverpool with protections which included the Isle of Man and Africa (see Appendix 2.15).

This document, however, was 'but little regarded'[18] and the crews could be impressed on each section of the triangular voyage. The *Will*, Hugh Crow captain, sailed in convoy with other Guinea ships from Liverpool in July 1801. She had a crew of nearly seventy men, including thirty-six able seamen who were 'qualified to take the wheel, being an uncommon proportion ... at a time when it was difficult to procure a good crew'. The convoy was in the South Channel, midway between the Old Head of Kinsale and the English coast when 'at daylight one morning, we had the misfortune, for so I must term it, to fall in with His Majesty's frigate *Amethyst* [Lieutenant Hill], from Cork, bound to Plymouth, with a small fleet of transports under her convoy'. The frigate's boats 'wantonly took from each of us a number of our ablest seamen' despite the protection. Crow told Hill 'that our little squadron would rather have fallen in with a French frigate of the same class than with the *Amethyst*'. Crow tried to get a message to his owner, Mr Aspinall, so that he could claim from the navy the advanced wages already paid to the men. The case failed because of a mistake in the name of the vessel or her commander.[4]

Table 10.1: Eighteenth Century War and Peace

1739-1743	War with Spain	
		10 years
1744-1748	War with France and Spain	
1749-1755	*Peace*	*7 years*
1756-1761	War with France	
		8 years
1762-1763	War with France and Spain	
1764 - 1775	*Peace*	*12 years*
1776 - 1777	War with America	
		7 years
1778 – 1782	War with America, assisted by France, Spain & Holland	
1783 – 1792	*Peace*	*10 years*
1793 – 1815	War with France	23 years

On Crow's final Guinea voyage, in 1807, the *Kitty's Amelia* was stopped in the Irish Sea by the *Princess Charlotte*, Captain Tobin. Despite her protection four of the vessel's ablest seamen were impressed. 'I felt on the occasion as if so many people had fallen overboard, whom I had not the power to assist, and my abhorrence of the impress service became, if possible, more firmly rooted'.[4]

Charles Christian, the surgeon on board the *William*, Richard Hart captain, stated that 'our original crew had all been transferred into the navy' in the West Indies. According to the *William*'s muster roll, on 8 January 1800 twenty-seven men were impressed on board HMS *Solebay*, the following day another eleven on HMS *Thunderer* and on 20 January another one on HMS *Greyhound*. They sailed from Jamaica with 'as motley a crew as could be; a turbulent and refractory sett – a mixture of Irishmen, Americans, Danes, and Frenchmen. Three were taken from the prison ship at Port Royal to give strength by their weakness'. Christian 'really expected that we should have been murdered'.[135]

At Jamaica, on 17 April 1801, a member of the crew on board the *Will*, Hugh Crow captain, was impressed on to HMS *Crescent*. Three days later seventeen of the crew deserted [recorded as 'run' on the muster roll].[136] Crow does not comment on this in his *Memoirs*. On 25 April eight more were actually impressed on HMS *Sherrad*. Only thirteen of the original crew of forty-two returned to Liverpool in July.

No Manxmen have been identified on any of these impressment lists. Thomas Kissag of Kirk Christ Lezayre but now belonging to Liverpool had been in the West Indies and 'there consequently time after time pressed to go into His Majesty's service in that troublesome part of the world'. As a result he was not able to claim the possessions belonging to his brother,

William, who had been a ship carpenter in Liverpool for several years. On his last trip home, the two brothers had spent time together and had 'several fraternal conversations'. During these William had 'by express words' declared that he wanted Thomas to be 'the sole executor of all his goods and effects in case he should happen to die'. Soon after this William went to sea and died abroad 'without making any alteration in his will and intention'. Now, in Thomas's enforced absence, their next of kin on the Isle of Man had been granted probate.

In August 1770 or 1771 Thomas Tear went on a Guinea voyage. He sent a letter to his wife, in Liverpool, telling her that he had been impressed on the English coast, during his homeward voyage. As she was dead, the letter was forwarded to Tear's mother, on the Island. She was also informed that her son's household goods and clothes were 'decaying' in their lodgings and that rent was still being charged. When a friend of the family went to Liverpool, he discovered that most of these things had been sold, to cover the rent. The few pieces of clothing that remained were brought back to the Island. As there was no more news of Thomas, his brother John had agreed to make further enquiries, when he was at London.[137]

Crow has the last word on this suject: 'The impressment of seamen I have always considered to be, in many points of view, much more arbitrary and cruel than what was termed the slave trade. Our great statesmen, however, are regardless of such evils at home, and direct their exclusive attention to supposed evils abroad'.

He had his own solution to the problem. 'If the wages of men of war's men were made equal to those given in the merchant service, and if small bounties were granted for volunteers for a certain number of years' service only, there can be no doubt but the navy would be more sufficiently manned than by the present system of coercion; and the expense of the impress service, with all its oppressions, would be saved to the country. The abolition of corporal punishments would also favour this object'.[4]

The Voyage of the *Duke of Argyle,* John Newton captain, 1750
Newton's Journal of this voyage provides useful information about the responsibilities put on his first mate, John Bridson, and also about the problems and dangers associated with obtaining the slaves. The *Duke of Argyle* sailed from Liverpool on 20 August 1750 and arrived at Frenchman's Bay in the river Sierra Leone at sunset on 23 October.

This whole area was extremely dangerous. There were sandbanks in the Sierra Leone river and along the coast. John Tear died here two years later, while second mate of the *Rose,* James Welch captain. As Welch wrote to the Consistory Court on the Island, Tear was on board the ship's boat going over the bar at the mouth of the Junk river, when it overturned and he was drowned. John Callister was on board the *Sarah* brig, Joseph Ward captain, in 1766. He died in the Casey River and Clement Chambers of Douglas, mariner saw his clothes thrown overboard immediately after he had been buried. The local natives could be untrustworthy. While the *Duke of Argyle* was on the coast they 'cut off' a French vessel, killing most of her crew. Newton was well aware that he was then sold some of the slaves originally purchased by the French.

Newton had been employed on the coast previously and he still had several contacts among the traders. As soon as the *Duke of Argyle* arrived, he made contact with these traders in an attempt to obtain his cargo quickly and to gain an advantage over all the other vessels trading on the coast at the same time. Once he had the promise of some slaves, Newton sent off the longboat with sufficient goods to purchase them. In the meantime he continued to negotiate other purchases either by going on shore to visit the traders himself or waiting until they approached him in one of their shallops.

As first mate, Bridson was in charge of the longboat. On 5 November 1750 he set out with goods to purchase eighteen slaves from Henry Tucker, the trader at Shebar (see Figure 10.1). Bridson went first to Whiteman's Bay in the Sierra Leone river and then to Plantanes for a pilot. They sailed for Sherbro Island on 8 November. Three weeks later Newton sent his yawl to Plantanes to find out if there was any news of the longboat. Bridson returned in another two days with eleven slaves and about a ton and half of camwood [also known as Afzel – Baphia nitida – a legume used for red dye].[138] The longboat was sent on shore with the carpenter for urgent repairs.

Bridson suggested that both the longboat and the yawl should go back to Sherbro immediately. He believed that large numbers of slaves would now be available there and no other Guinea vessels were currently on that part of the coast to compete for them. He had brought one of Tucker's men with him from Shebar to protect both the boats from the Sherbro natives.

At daylight on 29 November 1750 the carpenter returned from the shore with the longboat and at noon both she and the yawl set out. When there was no news of either of them for several days, on 10 December Newton sailed down to Shebar, where he fired three guns and hoisted the [Union] Jack to the fore topmast – the signal used for the boats to come back to the ship. The yawl did return, with three slaves who had been purchased by Bridson.

Newton was clearly disappointed by this small number of slaves and he went on shore himself. The problem appeared to be that Bridson's cargo was not well enough 'assorted' for the local market. As a result Newton sent John Hamilton, the third mate, back to the *Duke of Argyle* in the punt. He was to send the yawl on shore with some more appropriate items. The vessel, however, had disappeared, even though Hamilton searched at least two leagues to the seaward of where she had been anchored the previous day. Fortunately the *Duke of Argyle* returned, having drifted down the coast, because the crew left on board had been either asleep or neglectful.

On 13 December the longboat went to Jamaica, on Sherbro Island, with sufficient goods for the five slaves Newton had been told would be there for him. The yawl was sent to Henry Tucker at Shebar for a few days with the carpenter and Matthew Curfey [sic] the tailor on board, for his personal use. Bridson sent a letter to Newton on 16 December, explaining that he was still with Mr Tucker because a French boat had been plundered by the natives at Jamaica and Bridson was waiting for one of the locals, William Cumberbatch, to go there with him, as a protection. Bridson had supplied the French boat with some provisions.

At 4 p.m. on 10 January 1751 the longboat was seen between the vessel and the shore. The punt was sent to her and discovered that the crew were ill. It had taken them ten days to get from Shebar to Junk River. According to Bridson they would never have reached the *Duke of Argyle* without the assistance of the women slaves on board. They had only purchased eleven slaves and had buried one crew member. Bridson and the other three crew were all sick..

At first Bridson seemed to recover and Newton planned to send him out in the longboat again in a couple of days. But he had a relapse. The fever returned and his face became swollen and inflamed – the worst case that Newton had ever seen. Bridson died a little before midnight on 20 January 1751. Newton was particularly concerned because his death would slow down the purchase of slaves. His first mate had been 'very diligent and earnest in promoting the ship's interest', getting on well with the natives 'wherever I sent him'. Bridson was buried at sunrise the next day with the vessel's colours at half mast and fourteen minute guns fired.

John Hamilton, the 3rd mate, was now put in charge of the longboat. [Newton appears not to have trusted his 2nd mate, Samuel Marshall, with any responsibility]. On 16 January they went to Tabo-caney with enough goods to purchase two slaves but returned two days later because the trader who was supposed to be supplying them 'never went near'.

Thomas Bridson, an apprentice on the *Duke of Argyle*, was now on board the longboat. On 21 January they went to Kittam and Shebar with goods for fifteen slaves, returning on 22 February having only purchased five. As the supplies of slaves at Kittam seemed to be exhausted, the next day the longboat was sent to St Pauls river, for a maximum stay of three weeks. She was away for so long that Newton was surprised to see her again - at 10 a.m. on 28 March. The longboat reached the vessel at 2 p.m. and had seven slaves on board. Hamilton explained that he had been away for so long because the crew had become very sick in St Pauls river. Two had now recovered but two were still extremely ill, one 'at the point of death'. Thomas Bridson died at 5 a.m. the next morning. Newton did not comment on his funeral.[119]

Figure 10.1: Sierra Leone and the Gold Coast

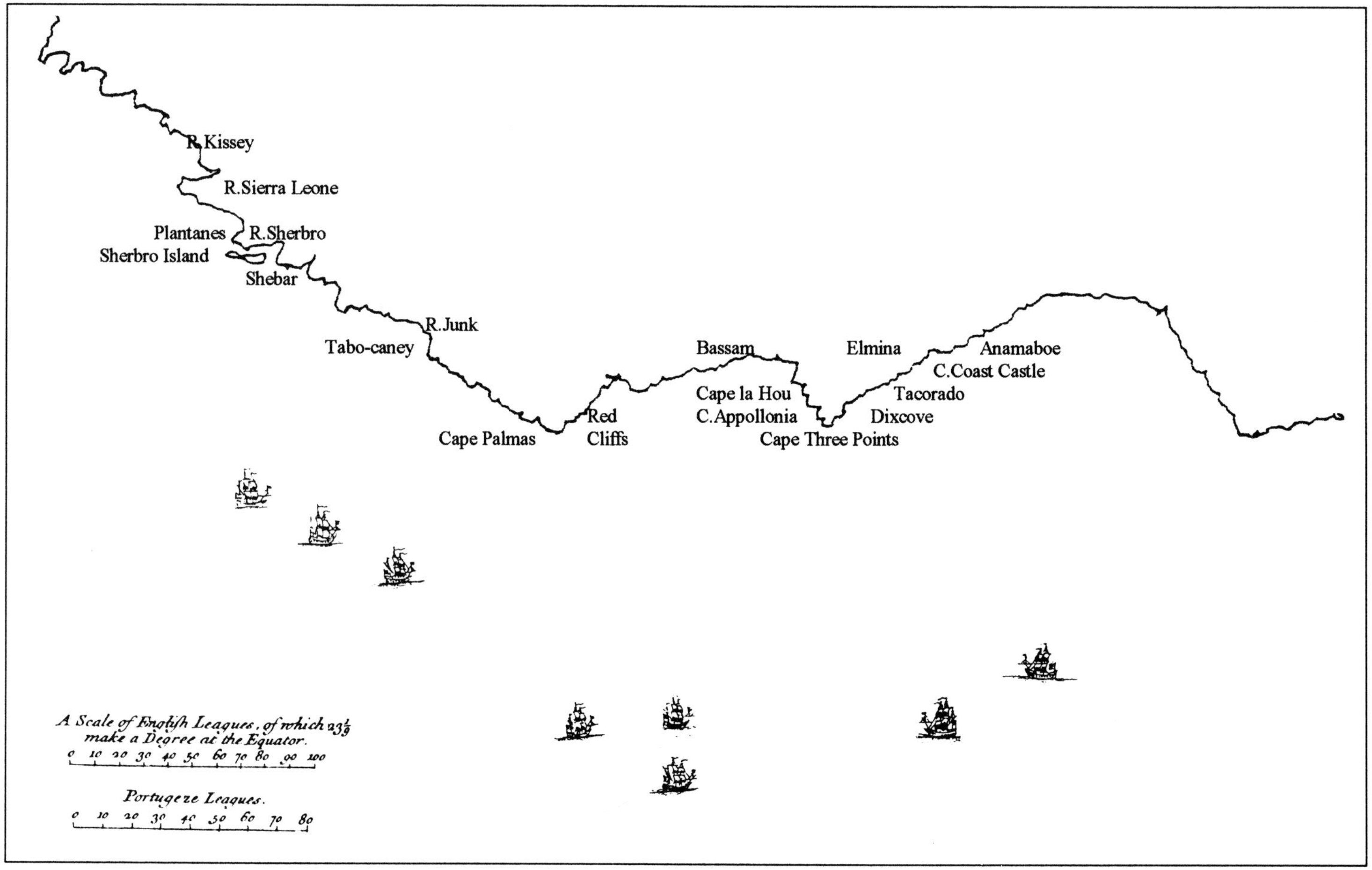

11

Manx Guinea Captains

John Carran

Over sixty Manx captains of Liverpool, Bristol and London Guinea vessels have been identified. It is impossible to estimate what fraction these represent of the total. Table 11.1 lists some Manx captains of Liverpool Guinea vessels, Hugh Crow's Guinea voyages are listed in Table 8.1 and Appendix 6 shows all the voyages undertaken by Ambrose Lace.

Table 11.1: Some Manx Captains of Liverpool Guinea Vessels

Lutwidge Affleck	William Gill
John Bean	William Gill
Christopher Brew	Philip Kewish
Henry Callow	Patrick Kewley
Thomas Cannell	Thomas Kewley
George Cannon	William Kewley
David Christian	Hugh Kissack
Ross Christian	Charles Kneal
Edward Clark	William Kneal
John Corran	Ambrose Lace
William Corran	William Lace
James Cosnahan	Alexander Lawson
Thomas Cottyman	Caesar Lawson
Hugh Cowell	William Lawson
Hugh Crow	Henry Moore
William Crow	John Quirk
Thomas Cubbon	Radcliffe Shimmins
Thomas Cubbon	Matthew Sibson
Edward Dugan	Francis Stowell
Quayle Fargher	James Stowell
George Farquhar	Thomas Stowell
William Farquhar	John Tear
John Finch	John Tobin
Michael Finch	Thomas Tobin
Henry Frissel	Daniel Vaughan
Richard Gawn	Robert Waterson
John Gill	

Note: This Table is based on the best information available at the time of going to press

Some of the Manx captains are well-known names: Hugh Crow and his *Memoirs* have been discussed already. He was described in *Manx Worthies* as 'the most famous of our merchant seamen'. Others named as 'more especially slavers' were Ambrose Lace, David Christian, William Crow, Edward Clarke and Radcliffe Shimmin.[139] Behrendt highlighted the Manx captains sailing from Liverpool and commented on David Christian in particular.[140] Harrison described the Mathematical School at Peel. This was founded by the Reverend James

87

Moore of Dublin, George Moore's brother, with the aim of teaching ten poor scholars 'gratis for ever, in the different branches' of mathematical science. There was a heavy bias towards navigation and the scholars educated there between April 1768 and February 1784 included Cannon and also Charles Kneal, John Quirk and Thomas Cannel.[141] In contrast there are the men like Henry Frissel and Thomas Cottyman, about whom nothing appears to have been written to date.

The Liverpool Trade and Shipping database, the Liverpool muster rolls and Behrendt's publications have been used as the source of statistical data about many of the Guinea captains. Frequently most information is available about them when they died - then they appear in the wills held either at the Manx Museum or at the Lancashire Record Office. As a result more is known about the deaths of many of these captains than their everyday lives.

There are exceptions. Information is available about Quayle Fargher's third and last Guinea voyage, as captain of the *Jane,* which sailed from Liverpool in 1786. Other Manx mariners on this vessel were John Quirk, who was to become a Guinea captain in his own right, Hugh Christian, William Harrison and John Clegg [Clague].[142] James Irving was also on board and his letters, which include both this voyage and the subsequent one, as captain of the *Anna* (see Chapter 8) have been published.[143] The 'Remarks on the Voyage of the *Ranger*, captain John Corran', describes what happened on board almost every day between December 1789, when the vessel left Lisbon, and September 1790 when she was about to leave Kingston (see Table 9.1, Table 11.2 and the section on the *Ranger* below).[122]

The Captains
Possibly as many as a third of the Manx captains died on board their vessels, either at sea or on the coasts of Africa and the West Indies. As will be seen, 'Died' is one of the commonest phrases in the muster rolls – no further details are given about the cause of death or on what part of the triangular voyage the death took place. It is possible to guess the whereabouts from the number of months and days since the vessel left Liverpool – but this may not necessarily be accurate.

Hugh Cowell was captain of the *Diana*, which sailed from Liverpool on 18 January 1790 with a crew of 32 men. According to her muster roll he was 'superceded by power of attorney' on 31 August 1790. It is supposed that he went insane and was confined at Cape Coast Castle – he died there in about 1803, intestate. The owners of the vessel sent Peter W Brancker to the Gold Coast to take over the command.[144]

William Crow, who was Hugh's brother, had escaped the explosion of the *Othello* at Bonny but he drowned there on 3 February 1800 during his second voyage as captain of the *Charlotte*. Another Manx mariner, Thomas Radcliffe, had died on 13 January (see Appendix 5). The vessel was taken from Africa to Trinidad by one of the mates, Chambers Reid, 'and then lost'. The surviving crew, including Edward Corkill and John Farquhar, were 'discharged' on 9 May. Michael Taylor, one of the owners of the vessel, completed the muster roll at Liverpool in November 1800.[145] Hugh Crow managed to obtain 'a good situation' in Jamaica for a second brother, John, a carpenter by trade. However he was drowned in 1802 'while on a party of pleasure near Kingston'.[4]

The possible death of the captain was always of great concern to the owners. Ambrose Lace was told 'in case of your mortality (which God forbid) your first mate, Mr Chapman, must succeed you in command'.[34] The chief mate, Mr Dugdale, was to take charge of the *Lottery* from Charles Kneal in an emergency 'but we hope you will enjoy good health and that you will have a short, happy and prosperous voyage'.[10]

When John Kelly, captain of the *Mary* died at Bonny, Thomas Cottyman became master of the vessel. She was spoken to near St Helena by the East Indiaman *Encount*, Captain Webber. He reported that 'the crew were very sickly, having buried above 100 slaves'.[146] This was Cottyman's only experience as captain of a slave vessel. He was drowned in December 1759 when the *Robert & Betty*, not in the Guinea trade, was lost on rocks in Madeira harbour.[16]

John Corran (see below) died in 1798 on his sixth Guinea voyage, as captain of the *Triton*. The chief mate, Francis Stowell, took over the vessel. She went to Demerara with her cargo of slaves, returning to Liverpool in November 1798. Stowell subsequently commanded two Guinea voyages. Another Manxman, Thomas Moore, was also on board the *Triton*.[147]

John Bean Hannay had been mate on board a vessel, the name appears to have been either the *Farmer* or the *James* – her muster roll has not been identified as yet – when the captain died on the Guinea coast. Hannay took command of the vessel. It was believed that his subsequent 'misconduct arose from (the indiscretion of youthful inexperience, having too soon the command of a large vessel with the disposal of the cargo) wishing to cultivate the good will of the chiefs on the coast of Africa, induced him to lend the assistance of his ship's boat etc to transport a few slaves over a river from one African chief to another'. Hannay knew that it was now illegal to trade in slaves but 'he did not think what he was doing constituted slave trading'. When Hannay returned to England 'on finding the nature of the offence he had committed <u>voluntarily</u> attended at Bow Street for the purpose of public examination'. Now he was in Newgate Prison awaiting transportation for seven years.[148] The date was 1817 – the slave trade had been abolished for ten years. No information has been found about what happened next. It is probable that Hannay was related to the Guinea captain John Bean.

<u>Family Connections</u>
The Crows were not the only brothers who were both Guinea captains. Other brothers included Charles and William Kneal, James and Thomas Stowell and John and Thomas Tobin. Ambrose Lace's son William was also in the Guinea trade. Caesar Lawson was William Lawson's son and the two Thomas Cubbins were father and son.

The name Kewley appears regularly as either captain of a Guinea vessel or one of the crew. John Kewley had been born and brought up in Liverpool before the family returned to the Island. On 9 September 1719 he was at Ramsey on board the *Standish* galley of Liverpool. He came on shore to tell his mother that he was bound on a voyage to Guinea and that he now had a wife at Liverpool, Catherine Skaasbrick. He died on that voyage (see Appendix 5). Daniel Kewley went to sea in the 1730s and after six years nothing more was heard of him so that he was presumed dead.

When Philip Kewley made his will in 1758, he described himself as a mariner of Liverpool. He was captain of six Guinea vessels: the *Boyn*, *Judith*, *Prince William*, *Racehorse*, *Peggy* and *Nelly* on six voyages between 1753 and 1764. When he died John Tarleton (IV) and his wife Alice were co-executors of his will.[149] Alice remarried - Alexander Lawson, another Guinea captain.

Thomas Kewley was captain of the *Prince Eugene* for four voyages from 1753 to June 1761, when the vessel was taken into Lisbon by a French privateer on her homeward voyage from Guadeloupe to Liverpool. His death was reported in the *Williamsons Liverpool Advertiser* dated 10 July: 'Captain Kewley, late commander of the *Prince Eugene* in the African trade, of the wounds he received in the engagement with a French privateer, a commander well respected amongst the merchants, traders, and all his acquaintance'.[150] It is believed that William Kewley, captain of the *Brooke*, was Thomas Kewley's son.

<u>Wealth</u>
It was possible for the Guinea captains to become wealthy men. Over and above their wages for the voyage they would collect various bonuses. They were allowed the value of a fixed number of the slaves sold 'on an average with the cargo'. In 1762 Ambrose Lace, as captain of the *Marquis of Granby*, was to receive the equivalent of ten slaves and his first mate and his surgeon two each. By 1802 the system had changed. Charles Kneal was to receive his coast commission from the West Indian merchant house 'who may sell your cargo of slaves'. This was £2 in £102 on the gross sales. After the chief mate and the doctor had received their 'privileges' Kneal would then have an additional commission of £4 in £104 of the remaining balance.[10]

The owners believed that these bonuses should be more than sufficient to satisfy the officers. Kneal was told that 'In consideration of the above emoluments neither you nor your crew nor any of them are directly or indirectly to carry on any private trade of receiving gratuities at Africa on your or their accounts under a forfeiture to us of the whole of your commissions arising on this voyage'.[10]

Crow reported on the successful voyage of his first Guinea command, the *Will* in 1798. 'I sold nearly £1200 worth of return goods, which I had saved from my outward cargo, and received the bounty allowed by government for the good condition of the slaves on their arrival'.[4]

Robert Waterson was captain of the *Africa* in April 1757 when she was lost in Carlisle Bay. The *Dove* and the *Duke of Cumberland* both arrived at Liverpool in May with part of her wrecked cargo of Guinea goods.[16] One wonders if any of it had been collected at the Isle of Man. This was Waterson's third voyage as captain. The other two voyages had been uneventful. His was captain on five more Guinea voyages: two on the *Snapper* and three on the *Essex*, of which he was co-owner.[16] There are no details of his death but his will was probated at Chester in 1766. He left Hannah, his wife, £200 plus all his household goods etc and the rest of his estate was to be converted into money, invested and used to educate his son. The total value of his estate is not known. His executors were 'my friends' Thomas Johnson and Thomas Foxcroft, both of whom were Guinea vessel owners.[151]

According to his brothers-in-law, John Corkan and Adam Cain, Hugh Kissack had sailed from the West Indies for home in November 1799 as captain of the *Penny* 'Guineaman'. He had been in company with two other vessels but had been separated from them and 'no account or intelligence having been received of or from him since it is therefore presumed that he has perished'. According to the muster roll in fact he drowned on 5 September 1799. The family believed that Kissack was 'possessed of property to a considerable amount'. His estate was less than £2,000.[152]

Several Manx captains retired to the Isle of Man and invested their capital in property. Hugh Crow converted East Ballaterson farm between Maughold and Ramsey into Crowville(a), which is still a working farm today. When Kneal returned to the Island, he purchased Raggat Farm [the Raggat], Ballaturson and Close Beg from Charles Cooper and Cronk Willin from William Graves of Peel. These properties were left to his mother and sister.

When Quayle Fargher returned to the Island after his last voyage, his friends were described as being 'joyful'. In 1787 he purchased Snugborough from Patrick Kelly, coroner of the Middle Sheading. The property had belonged to George Moore's brother Philip, who owned the nearby estate of the Hills. Moore had settled the property on his son Philip, who died at Leghorn. In the meantime Moore senior had used Snugborough as security against a loan of £500 Irish. The coroner sold the property to recoup the money. After Fargher was dead, Philip junior's eldest daughter, Eunice Caterine Theresa Moore, and her husband went to court in an attempt to reclaim Snugborough – they reckoned that the loss of the property had damaged them by at least £10,000. Fargher's widow managed to retain the property. It remained in the joint ownership of Esther Fargher and Mark Quayle her brother [both Esther and Mark were children of the merchant William Quayle].[153] Fargher is also listed in Jefferson's Manx Almanack for 1808 as owning Shen-Valley in Malew parish. He died at the Abbey, Malew. Christopher Brew, who died in 1799, had purchased Close e Chonoly in Christ Kirk Lezayre parish and Creg in Ballaugh.[154]

Radcliffe Shimmin 'departed this life suddenly' without settling his affairs. Most of his estate consisted of cash stored in the house together with details of his investments. His widow, living in Liverpool, had hoped that an account would be made of everything 'for the safety and satisfaction of all persons concerned'. Instead immediately after his death his 'next relations' took the keys of his desks and other places where the money, securities, title deeds and other valuable papers were stored. She appointed Thomas Stowell her attorney. Despite careful accounting each of the children only received £30.

The Voyage of the *Ranger*, John Corran captain, 1798-1790

The *Ranger* sailed from Liverpool in November 1789. She appears to have put into Lisbon for repairs. The remarks on her voyage, probably written by Ladwick Carlile, her first mate, start at Lisbon in early December. They record the distance travelled, the weather and amount of sail used. From 7 to 21 December the *Ranger* covered 1894 miles i.e. an average of 110 miles per day. There is then a gap and the record starts again on 1 January 1790. From then until landfall on 13 January she covered another 620 miles at an average rate of 50 miles per day. There are also comments about the work being undertaken by the crew (see Table 11.2)

On the Coast of Africa

The crew spent the last part of the outward voyage and much of their time on the African coast preparing for the slaves coming on board. They erected netting, to prevent them from jumping overboard (but see below) and a barricado to divide the deck so that the slaves would be kept separate from the crew. In the meantime purchase of slaves was very slow. In the first month they only received twenty-one on board.

Supplies were a constant concern. The crew made several trips to bring water by sea from Cape Coast Castle and collecting wood to be used as fuel for cooking. When the *Ranger* left the African coast she had on board: 73 puncheons and 16 gang casks of water, 600 crues of beans, 90 crues of rice, 357 crues of corn and 6,500 billets of wood.

The Middle Passage

The *Ranger*'s journey is described in Chapter 8. By 29 June some of the slaves were complaining of 'a gripping in the belly'. The same problem was reported on 6 July. Otherwise there were regular comments about the slaves being in 'good spirits' – on 11 July, 19 July, 21 July, 24 July, 10 August, 12 August, 17 August and 20 August. A man slave 'that slept in the boys' room attempted to cut his throat with a knife or some other instrument and at daylight on 7 July 1790, when the hatch was taken off to get the tubs, the slave came upon deck and jumped overboard but was picked up with the boat and is in a fair way of recovery'. Only three slaves appear to have died during the middle passage: on 20 July one man, cause unknown (he was reported as having a health problem the day before); 14 August one man, of a mortification in the leg and 21 August one woman, of the flux.

By 5 August the crew were catching storm water on deck to supplement the dwindling supplies. When they arrived at Barbados they had only 41 buckets and 5 gang casks of water left and the wood supply was reduced to 2,643 billets. Corran went on shore and returned with limes, oranges and plantains.

At the West Indies
The *Ranger* arrived at Kingston on 23 August 1790. Some of the slaves were sent ashore two days later and those who were not sold were returned to the ship. A woman slave died of pleurisy on 28 August.

On 1 September 1790 there was a severe storm at Kingston and 'several vessels drifted ashore in different places in the harbour'. The *Ranger* lost the rudders off both boats and these, together with other damage, were repaired the next day. On 18 September 1790 she took on board 9 tons of ballast and 10 barrels of bread. Two days later there were only 12 slaves unsold. The remarks end here.

The crew
According to the muster roll, when Corran sailed from Liverpool there were twenty-four crew on board.[155] Only twelve of these completed the voyage but none of them had died. Before the remarks started, two had 'run' on 2 December 1789, presumably at Lisbon.

Inevitably problems could easily develop on board if the crew were allowed to get drunk. As Caesar Lawson's instructions, in 1803, stated 'do not suffer drunkenness among any of your officers or crew, for it is sure to be attended with some misfortune, such as insurrection, mutiny and fire'.[156] On Sunday, 31 January 1790 Christian Freeze and George Hall [or Hill] were working with the second mate, Henry Woods, in the hold, where the rum was stored. While Woods was 'obliged to leave them' alone, Freeze and Hall embezzled some of the rum and as a result became intoxicated. Corran overheard Freeze bestowing 'illiberal and mutinous language' to Woods and when he tried to intervene he also received 'abusive and ill language'. As punishment, Corran ordered that Freeze and Hall's daily rum allowance should be withdrawn 'until the expiration of eight days'.

The rum continued to cause problems. On Friday, 19 February Daniel Chieves behaved in a mutinous manner to Mr Woods and the boatswain confessed that 'all the people on board' had been involved in embezzling rum. As things were clearly getting out of hand, Corran went up to Cape Coast Castle to make a complaint to the naval commodore there 'against the people for breaking into the hold'. He was told that the 'supposed ringleaders and mutineers' could be transferred to the naval ship. She arrived at Anamaboe Roads on 22 February and Sampson Thrust and Daniel Chieves were put on board 'for the safety of the vessel and cargo'. According to the muster roll Chieves and Thrust were both 'discharged' on 20 February.

On 20 March the rum was replaced, when four puncheons were traded for two women slaves and a small anchor. Two days after the *Ranger* arrived at Kingston, George Hill, James Haselden, Robert Pattison and John Palmer went 'upon duty ashore' in the boat and refused to return to the vessel because they 'did not approve' of the second mate's conduct towards them and 'for that reason were resolved to quit the vessel'. The next day the four seamen came on board with 'the Lieutenant', presumably based at Kingston, to collect their clothes etc. According to the muster roll all four were 'discharged' on 24 August 1790.

At 12 noon on 29 August 1790 a man of war's boat came alongside and 'enquired if any of the people were inclined to enter into His Majesty's naval service'. John Damarrin 'acquiesced with the request'. As this appeared to be a voluntary move on Damarrin's part, it was recorded that he had been 'discharged' and not impressed.

There were two other problems with the *Ranger*'s crew at Kingston. On 4 September William Grahame, the third mate, went on shore but 'declined returning to the vessel. The reason for such conduct is yet entirely unknown'. He was also recorded as 'discharged'. Then at 5.00 p.m. on 18 September, James Turner got liberty from Mr Woods to go ashore for three hours and never returned. He is described as having 'run'.

On 9 September 1790 Corran sent John Danials and John Critchlow [Critchley] to the hospital at Kingston. Their fate is not known, as they were also recorded as having been 'discharged'. Three new crew were taken on board at Jamaica. The *Ranger* returned to Liverpool on 25 November 1790. Christian Freeze was still on board.

According to his will, dated 24 May 1794, Corran left £40 to his mother, Margaret, a widow now living in Liverpool, all the household goods etc to his wife, another Margaret, and the residue of his estate to Henry Harrison, potpainter, and Anthony Troutbeck, clothier, both of Liverpool, to hold in trust for his children. Both his wife and Henry Harrison died and Troutbeck 'renounced' any involvement in the will. It was 1821 before the final administration (valued at £1,500) was completed by Corran's daughter, Matilda, described as a spinster of Speke (see Figure 2.1).[157]

Table 11.2: The *Ranger*'s Logbook: Lisbon to the Gold Coast
Employment of the crew

Date	Employment
5 December 1789	Making mats for the lower yards sinet and other needful jobs
7 December 1789	In the hold and making mats for the rigging and yards. Cooper making hoise buckets
8 December 1789	Making sinet. Carpenter fitting cranes of the boat. Cooper making hoise buckets etc as needful
13 December 1789	In sundry jobs about the rigging
14 December 1789	In making gaskets and points
16 December 1789	In making points, gaskets, swabs etc
17 December 1789	Making points for the new topsail. Cooper making crues. Carpenter fitting cranes for the yoal
18 December 1789	Making sinet, fitting the new fore topsail and knotting yarns
19 December 1789	Making matts for the shrouds and middle sticking the fore top sail
20 December 1789	Sundry jobs. Carpenter building the necessary
21 December 1789	Reducing main sail and making matts for the shrouds. Cooper making crues. Carpenter as usual
1 January 1790	Sundry jobs about the rigging of the boat
2 January 1790	Squaring the ratlings of the top mast rigging and fitting the quarter deck annwaning [awning]
3 January 1790	Making sinet swabs and middle sticking the foresail. Carpenter in sundry jobs about the long boat. Cooper making hoise buckets, crues etc
4 January 1790	Clearing the decks. Carpenter about sundry jobs about the long boat [which appears to have been being towed astern]
5 January 1790	Getting the anchors over the bows and cables ready for bonding
6 January 1790	Knotting yarns and middle sticking foresail
7 January 1790	Making and taking in sail
8 January 1790	Making rope for quarter deck netting, middle sticking the main stay sail. Carpenter fitting the necessary
9 January 1790	Making ropes for netting and middle sticking the main staysail
10 January 1790	Painting the boats and other necessary jobs
11 January 1790	Sundry jobs as needful
12 January 1790	Making the quarter deck netting and other jobs as needful
13 January 1790	Painting the ship. Carpenter fitting the barricado
15 January 1790	Painting the ship. Carpenter fitting the barricado
18 January 1790	People employed in necessary jobs. Carpenter building the barricado
19 January 1790	Carpenter and people employed as yesterday

Notes:
i.   The *Ranger* left Lisbon on 7 December 1789 & arrived at Anamaboe Road on 19 January 1790
ii. Source: Remarks on the voyage of the *Ranger*[122]

The *Sailor's Word-Book*[18] gives some information about these various tasks:

Crue: another word for kreel – a framework of timber for the catching of fish. In this instance it is believed that a crue was a small bowl (see Chapter 15)

Hoise is the old word for hoist. It is believed by the author that hoise buckets were used for pulling the water out of the hold in the Middle Passage..

Gasket: a cord or piece of plaited stuff, to secure furled sails to the yard, by wrapping it three or four times round both, the turns being at a competent distance from each other

Mats: To prevent chafing, a thick mat is woven from strands of old rope, spun yarn, or foxes, containing each a greater or lesser number of rope yarns , in proportion to the intended mat to be made.

Pointing: the operation of unlaying and tapering the end of a rope, and weaving some of its yarns about the diminished part, which is very neat to the eye, prevents it from being fagged out, and makes it handy for reeving in a block etc.

Ratling: another word for ratlines – small lines which traverse the shrouds of a ship (at distances of 15 or 16 inches) horizontally from the deck upwards, and are made firm by jamming clove-hitches; they form a series of steps, like the rounds of a ladder.

Sinet [sinnet/sennit] a flat cordage formed by plaiting five or even rope yarns together. Straw, plaited in the same way for hats, is called plat-sennit; it is made by sailors in India from the leaf of the palm, for that well-known straw-hat, adorned with flowing ribbons, which formerly distinguished the man-of-war's man.

Swab: a sort of long mop, formed of rope-yarns of old junk, used for cleaning and drying the decks and cabins of a ship.

Barricado: was the barrier constructed between the slaves quarters and the rest of the vessel.

12

The Guinea Surgeons

Cha.ᵉ Christian

Every Guinea vessel carried a surgeon - their task was not an easy one as they had to cope with the wide range of illnesses that afflicted both the crew and the slaves in the tropics. As Hugh Crow wrote, very few of the Guinea crews had been in a warm climate before and if they became ill 'they seldom recovered, though every attention was paid to them'.[4] Between 1700 and 1807 over sixty Manx mariners died 'on the coast of Guinea' (see Appendix 5). Though not all of these died from sickness, a common jingle was:

> 'Beware and take care
> Of the Bight of Benin;
> For one that comes out,
> There are forty go in'[158]

Crow was second mate of the *Jane*, Reuben Wright captain, which sailed from Liverpool in 1792. 'Having completed our cargo of about four hundred blacks we set sail, after a stay at Bonny of five months, during which we lost several of our crew, and some slaves'.[4]

There are not many instances in the will microfilms where the exact details of a mariner's death are given. While there are several letters referring to the death of Daniel Cottiman, cooper on board the *Salisbury*, Thomas Marsden captain, they simply informed his mother that her son was 'dead' (see Chapter 10).

Richard Cole of Ramsey is an exception. He made his will in April 1756 before going to sea. It appears that he died on his first Guinea voyage as crew on board the *Sea Nymph*, William Parkerson captain. During the Middle Passage from Africa to Barbados, he was 'seized with a mortification in his legs'. When the vessel reached the West Indies Cole was sent on shore with 'others in disorder' and died there in April 1757. James Singleton, the *Sea Nymph*'s boatswain, reported to the Manx Consistory Court that as he could not be 'actually present upon shore' he did not see Cole dead or buried but believed him not to be alive 'by his information from the nurse, doctor and those belonging to the hospital'.

Similarly the muster rolls simply record that a mariner had 'died' on a particular date. Sometimes there is a distinction between having died and having drowned but it would be unsafe to assume that all those who died had been ill first. In the case of the large number of deaths on board the *Kitty's Amelia*: half of the crew died on her last voyage – 23 out of a total of 45 – there are some comments from Hugh Crow. He wrote that these deaths were 'attributable to the culpable neglect of others, the consequences of which we could neither foresee nor control'.[4] The problem was that in the rush to prepare the *Kitty's Amelia* so that she could sail before the official end of the slave trade neither the vessel nor some of the returned cargo had been cleaned and aired properly after her previous voyage, when there had been sickness on board. Two mariners who were possibly Manx, Peter Corlett, a seaman, and Allin

Christian, a sailmaker, both died on 2 January 1808, having been on board for 5 months and 8 days.[159]

Some of the most useful information about sickness on the Sierra Leone coast comes from Newton's Journal.[119] Edward Lawson was an ordinary seaman on board the *Duke of Argyle* and he had been sent out with Bridson in the longboat to purchase slaves (see Chapter 10). In December he was taken back on board the vessel, ill with a fever. He died on 18 December 1750 and Newton noted that it was necessary to bury him immediately, as he was 'extremely offensive'. Lawson appears in the Manx records: according to the Consistory Court held at Andreas on 16 March 1769, he had died on the Guinea coast 'about 18 years ago'.

The role of the surgeon was extremely important not only in keeping the crew alive but also in treating any sickness amongst the slaves. As Calabar was 'remarkable for great mortality in slaves', Ambrose Lace of the *Marquis of Granby* was instructed by his owners that as: 'We desire you may take every prudent method to prevent it [mortality]. Viz. not to keep your ship too close in the day time and at night time to keep the ports shut as the night air is very pernicious'.[34] The surgeon also had to keep the slaves as well as possible during the Middle Passage.

Several of the surgeons, like the one on Charles Kneal's *Lottery*, received head money of 1s for each slave sold. When the *William*, Richard Hart captain, was nearly lost in the Congo river, Christian the surgeon commented that 'This disaster threw the ship into such confusion, and occasioned so much uncleanliness and mephitic effluvium as to cause the death of many slaves. I was grieved and much disappointed, because I had expected that the captain and myself would have gained, and been triumphant by, the premium the Act of Parliament in its wisdom to encourage humanity allowed to the captain £100, and to the surgeon £50, if so many were purchased, and so few died before an arrival in port for sale'.[135]

Crow was highly critical of this regulation. 'Could any one in his senses suppose, that after paying perhaps £25 for a negro, their owners would not take especial care of them, and give them those comforts which would conduce to their health? Many a laugh I and others have had at Mr. Wilberforce and his party, when we received our hundred pounds bounty'.[4]

Manx Surgeons
Four Manx surgeons have been identified on Guinea vessels:

Charles Christian was surgeon on board the *William*, Richard Hart captain (see below).[160]

Peter Miller was surgeon on board the *Dart*, Edward Crosby captain.[161] She sailed from Liverpool in January 1802 and returned there in February 1804, having taken on a new crew in the West Indies and gone to Africa a second time before returning to Liverpool. Miller died at Africa in March 1802, having been on board for 1 month and 27 days. He was the first person on board to die. Although the Place of Abode column is completed, there is no evidence of any other Manxmen on board. Table 12.1 refers to the first voyage and not the new crew, which does not appear to have included a surgeon. The first mate, John Woolrich, of Farnworth, Cheshire, was discharged at Demerara. In February 1806 Woolrich called at Ramsey, now captain of a vessel, the *Harriet*. He made his will on the Island and died on the Guinea coast later that year.

Robert Patton was surgeon on board the *Dick*, George Irvin captain.[162] She sailed from Liverpool in September 1802 and returned to London in August 1803. Robert Patton died at

Surinam on 10 May 1803, having been on board for 7 months and 15 days. He was the tenth person to die on the ship. The Place of Abode is recorded as Liverpool for the whole crew. There were no other recognisably Manx crew on board.

Phillip Garrett was surgeon on board the *Ceres*, Adam Elliott captain.[132] She sailed from Liverpool in April 1804 and returned in July 1805. In addition to the captain there was a crew of 41 (see Table 12.1). There were five other Manx mariners on board:

Name	Position	Fate	Date
William Teare	Mate	Completed the voyage, returning to Liverpool	5 July 1805
John Kelly	Carpenter	Impressed	22 December 1804
William Corkhill	Joiner	Impressed	12 December 1804
John Killop	Landsman	Entered the navy	28 January 1805
Paul Bridson	Tailor	Died	10 January 1805

Because of the number of the original crew who had 'run' from the ship, 10 additional seamen were taken on at Jamaica. Six of these died on the homeward voyage. Garrett was discharged at Liverpool on 5 July 1805.

Table 12.1: Manx Surgeons and their Voyages

Vessel	*William*	*Dart*	*Dick*	*Ceres*
Captain	Richard Hart	Edward Crosby	George Irvin	Adam Elliott
Surgeon	Charles Christian	Peter Miller	Robert Patton	Phillip Garrett
Total Crew	49	21	27	41
Died	3	7 (all at Africa)	6 (Africa) 5 (Surinam) 2 (at sea)	5 1 discharged 'sick'
Drowned	2			
Impressed	40		2	18
Entered Navy			1 (Dutch service)	1
Run				8
Discharged en route		2 (Africa) & 1 (Demerara)	1 (Ireland)	2
Discharged at end of voyage	4	11 (Antigua)	10 (London)	6

The Voyage of the *William*, Richard Hart captain and Charles Christian surgeon[135]
Born in 1762, Christian trained at the Medical School in Edinburgh before sailing as surgeon on board the *Middlesex* East Indiaman. After several years back in England he suffered a fit of melancholy, aggravated by drinking. He gave up his lucrative medical practice in Leicester and went to Birmingham where he lived for two years. 'My brother paid me a visit there and advised me to come to the Island and live with my mother. To this I felt the most extreme repugnance … when I had arrived at Liverpool, my aversion to coming grew more forcible'. He convinced his brother that he should go on a Guinea voyage instead of to the Isle of Man. On 5 February 1799 Christian was certified by the Liverpool Medical Board as a surgeon for the slave trade.

Christian sailed in this vessel sailed from Liverpool on 20 February 1799. Other members of her crew included Thomas Walker, first mate, and Robert Warbrick, second mate. Problems developed between Christian and Warbrick and these tend to dominate his account of the voyage. There are very few references to sickness on board.

The *William* appears to have purchased all her slaves in the river Congo area. Both the captain and the first mate would travel large distances up river, to make contact with the inland slave traders. Walker returned from one of these trading trips 'enfeebled by the endemic fever'. His cot was suspended on the quarter deck so that he could benefit from the fresh air and Christian put an awning over him 'to guard against what I deemed the noxious influence of the night damp'. Yet during the night 'someone' threw the awning aside, leaving Walker 'free and open exposure to the chill dew of the night'. Christian went on deck unusually early the next morning only to find the first mate 'lying in a stupor, openly exposed'. He died on 15 June 1799. Christian clearly suspected that Warbrick had hastened Walker's death by removing the awning. As soon as Walker became ill, Warbrick was overheard claiming that he would now receive the equivalent value of two slaves instead of one.

The *William*'s Middle Passage appears to have been uneventful. The Guinea vessels often had to stay in the Americas for several months, waiting for their cargoes to be sold. Christian reported: 'We lay upwards of three months at Kingston. The captain had lost my esteem by his too frugal treatment of us while we lay there. It perhaps might deserve a more harsh term. He provided this mate and myself beef .. and nothing else excepting some vegetables during the whole time, and left us to purchase tea, coffee, rolls, rum and sugar from our own pockets. The mate all this time was more profuse in every respect in his expenditure that I was. How was much of that money procured? I learnt that our plan of providing was very different from that of other surrounding ships in the same service'.

Encounters with the Enemy
Before leaving Jamaica, the *William* and two other armed Guineamen agreed to sail from Port Royal 'in company as convoy to each other'. The other two vessels sailed on time but 'our strength of hands could not effect the purpose'. By the time the *William* was reunited with the others, one had been wrecked on a small uninhabited island between Jamaica and St Domingo and the other had been in a 'severe engagement with a Spanish privateer full of men'.

Christian was invited on board the other vessel by her surgeon. He was deeply affected by the scene 'never having had opportunity before to witness the horrid effects of warfare, - men fighting with men to conquer or die. My admiration of their courage was raised to the highest pitch, and the deplorable situation the whole crew were then in made me shudder at

great victory ... There were few on board but what had received wounds of a more or less dangerous nature. A gentleman – a passenger – was in his cot, who had escaped bodily injury, but who had fought hard, and was then in a violent fever from the wounds he had received in his mind – from killing and the danger of being killed'. This vessel was 'unable to keep company with us and where they went and what their fate was, that I have never heard. Their names I knew not, ship or captain'.

Less than a week away from Liverpool, in late 1800 the *William* was captured by *Le Brave*, apparently without putting up a fight. Everyone was taken on board the privateer, except Christian and the mate, Warbrick, who stayed on the *William* with two French officers and twenty men. Instead of going to Bordeaux, which was the *Le Brave*'s home port, they went to Corunna in Spain.

'The two French officers behaved to us in the most extreme degree of kindness. I think they found no rum on board, but luckily two pipes of Madeira were discovered – one of these was placed on legs in the cabin and a common turncock put into it. We were permitted to drink as much as ever we pleased of it, on condition that we gave not a drop to the men; they had their regular and stinted supply. Two or three turtles were dressed; we fared sumptuously'.

as much as ever we pleased of it, on condition that we gave not a drop to the men; they had their regular and stinted supply. Two or three turtles were dressed; we fared sumptuously'.

After about a week 'We were then sent off through a part of Spain and a part of Portugal to Oporto, accompanied by three common sailors – one an Englishman who had been left behind sick, belonging to a prior captured party – and two Americans, from whence or how they sprung I cannot say'. Warbrick had the joint passport in his pocket. He succeeded in leaving Christian behind in a village where they had stopped for refreshment. Christian 'proceeded onwards for two days without him, and arrived at a garrison town situated on the river Minho – Tuy, its name I think. On the opposite side of the river is a town of the same description in Portugal. This river divides the two nations'. There was no sign of a party of seamen. Christian explained his problem to the governor and was quartered at a small inn for two days. 'I happened to have some small instruments in my pocket for teeth cleaning. A monastery fronted this house on the other side of the street. I became known to some of the monks, and made a little money by exercising the art of a dentist'.

At last Warbrick and the others arrived, having lost their way and gone to Vigo, where they had been 'put into the guard-room during one night'. The party now crossed into Portugal and went to Viana, where they contacted the English consul, Mr Allen. He found them quarters in the town but soon Christian moved in with the Allen household. 'I continued at their house seven weeks, and was treated with as much civility the last day as the first'. Allen 'voluntarily supplied me with more money than was allowed by our government to prisoners of war'. Christian met Captain Bradford at the house. Because he had 'violently inflamed eyes; he consulted me I benefited him, and he gave me in consequence my passage to England, living comfortably with him instead of being subjected to the noisy bustle of a man of war. I was landed at Deal'.[135]

Crow dedicated a whole chapter of his Memoirs to the *Gregson*'s encounter with a French privateer in July 1794. Crow was chief mate and the vessel only had a crew of 35 men compared with 150 on board the *Robuste*, which had 'twenty-four long twelve-pounders'. After nearly two hours 'much of our rigging being cut to pieces, and several of our people being severely wounded, we reluctantly surrendered, as to continue the action would only have been to throw our lives uselessly away'.

The crew were taken into the French port of L'Orient, where they spent a few weeks as prisoners of war and had 'no reason to complain of our treatment'. In August they were marched to Quimper, where they joined several thousand other prisoners. Here the conditions were appalling. Their daily ration was one and a half pounds of bread, which was 'black and clammy ... so execrable that we could hardly endure the smell of it' and 'two very small fish called "sardaigns", which hardly made a mouthful'. The prison commander was 'little better than an unfeeling madman'.

By the middle of November 1794 nearly two thousand of the prisoners had died. Those who were still able to walk were marched in gangs of fifty through civil war ravaged France towards the north. Sometimes they had to sleep in ruined churches or noblemen's houses and at 'other times in dirty stables' One day they might march twenty to twenty-five miles only to have to retrace their steps the next 'owing to the disturbed state of the country'.

After he had marched five or six hundred miles Crow was too ill to continue and so was hospitalised at Pontoise about the end of February 1795 [had they walked in a straight line then the distance between Quimper and Pontoise would have been about 290 miles]. Here he found some English prisoners, including the mate of a ship 'who gave me great assistance in acquiring a better knowledge of arithmetic, and of navigation by means of logarithms, which I found to be of the greatest benefit to me in after life'.

At the beginning of May 1795 Crow 'contrived to elude the vigilance of my keepers' and escaped. After various adventures, including close encounters with French soldiers, he finally reached Havre de Grace [Le Havre]. Here he obtained a passage to Deal on board a Danish ship. Having 'kissed the soil of my native country, grateful for my return after so many hardships' Crow borrowed sufficient money to return to Liverpool – after an absence in prison of twelve months.[4]

Both Crow and Christian had returned to Deal but their ordeals had been very different. Crow's Memoirs continue the story of his life. Very little is known about Christian after he returned to the Island. Richard Hart, who had been captain of the William, died in the Congo river in May 1803, when captain of the *Otter* on his fifth Guinea voyage. The second mate, Robert Warbrick, became a Guinea captain and died on his second voyage, when commander captain of the *Minerva* in June 1804.[140]

Conclusion

It cannot be disputed that the Isle of Man was involved in the Atlantic slave trade – from the supply of Guinea goods before Revestment to the increasing numbers of Manx mariners on board the slave ships in all phases of the triangular voyages.

There has always been some appreciation of the Island's 'warehouse' role for Guinea cargoes, from the Scottish Board of Customs response to the Treasury Enquiry in 1764 to the present day, but the range of these goods has not been fully recognised. For example, the cargo lists for the *Scipio* and the *Peace galley* are in the Liverpool Port Books at the PRO, but it is now clear that these basic lists were supplemented with an entirely different range of goods collected at Ramsey.

These cargoes were probably far bigger than has been appreciated to date. The sheer volume of East India goods that was imported into the Island changes our calculations of the total values of the cargoes going to the Guinea coast from England. In most cases the exact value of these additional goods in a cargo is not known, but the Davenport accounts do provide some examples. On one occasion several hundred pounds worth of beads were collected from Hugh Cosnahan at Douglas. The total volume of goods leaving Liverpool and the north-west ports needs to be supplemented by an estimate of the Manx contribution.

Previous analyses have been made of the total number of guns exported from England as part of the Guinea trade. These calculations do not take account of the large numbers of guns available on the Island. It is interesting that Walter Lutwidge's cargo list specifically stated that the guns must be English made as Dutch guns would not do, yet the Manx customs entries indicate that there was actually a sizeable market for these Dutch guns.

Several merchant networks have emerged – Richard Gildart and Foster Cunliffe were apparently the first Liverpool merchants to send their Guinea vessels to the Island for parts of their cargoes. The Tarletons were not far behind. The Tarleton theme continues for several years – from importations specifically for 'Mr Tarleton & Co' to vessels either captained by or unloaded by a Tarleton. The Duke of Atholl used John IV as his banker in Liverpool, and the same Tarleton intervened over the seizure of a gunpowder vessel by a Scottish revenue boat.

The Tarletons were responsible for some high value importations of Guinea goods. There were seventy of these 'large importations' by non-Manx merchants etc. It should be comparatively simple to follow through the Tarleton link to the name of the Guinea vessel involved. Further investigation is required in an attempt to identify where the Guinea vessels came from that collected the other 'large importations'.

Some of the merchants importing the Guinea goods were either Irish or Scottish. It is still not completely clear how much their presence involved the 'band wagon' of supplying the

English vessels and how much it masked slave ships from these countries calling at the Island and then sailing for Guinea.

From time to time the British government took sporadic action against the Manx Guinea trade – George Dow of the Whitehaven *Sincerity* revenue cruiser attempted to seize the *Hope* dogger in 1750 with East India goods on board, and Arthur Onslow did seize at Liverpool in 1763 the three vessels that had been loaded by the Hopes in Rotterdam. If there had been a more consolidated attack rather than these individual interventions the revenue might have made a greater impact earlier than 1764. At this point the 'principal' merchants on the Island complained strongly to the Duke of Atholl about the 'recent' depredations by the English and Irish revenue cruisers. These attacks were beginning to 'terrify' the Liverpool merchants and without Liverpool's backing that side of the Island's trade certainly would have disappeared.

There were a number of merchant failures. The Reeves brothers were not the only ones to go out of business deeply in debt. It is impossible to disentangle which of these debts related to the Guinea trade, which to smuggling and which to some more legal occupations. Had the Island not been purchased by the Crown it is a matter for speculation what might have happened. Could there have been enough business failures to destroy sufficient of the financial structure for the 'trade' in prohibited goods to end anyway?

Our understanding of the logistics of the rum trade is challenged by the large quantities of rum that were brought to the Island by way of the Guinea trade. It is now clear that slaving subsidised smuggling. This dropping off point for the homeward cargoes also alters some of the previous concepts about the return cargoes of the slaving vessels. In other words they came from the West Indies with a higher valued cargo on board than had been reckoned.

The number of Manxmen on board the Guinea vessels, in all capacities from mariner to captain, was larger than had been expected given the small population of the Island. Certainly there would have been surplus mariners available during the years immediately after Revestment, when employment on the smuggling wherries was no longer a major alternative to herring fishing or farming.

Hugh Crow is well-known. The impression is often given that he was the slave captain from the Isle of Man – but over the century there were more than fifty of them sailing from Liverpool alone. Many of their detailed careers are as yet unknown. It would be particularly interesting to know how they, and the merchants, invested their profits from the Guinea trade – and what sums these profits represented.

Charles Christian was one of four Manx surgeons identified on the Guinea vessels. Little is known of his career after the voyage of the *William* and his visit to the Island to see his mother. Were there many more Manx surgeons at sea? How large a role did they play in the East Indian and West Indian trades as well as in the Guinea trade? How many naval surgeons were there? Where did they all train?

The Next Stage
There are several points in the book when the phrase 'work continues' or 'work is ongoing' would have been appropriate. This section outlines the future plans.

Extracts from the archive material used in the research for this book, analyses of this information and datasets on CDROM of the Manx customs entries for Guinea goods, mariners deaths etc will be lodged at the Manx National Heritage library. They will be supplemented by new information as this becomes available. This material will form the foundation for a continued study of the Island's role in the Atlantic slave trade. The questions raised in the conclusion will be considered in the future as part of the ongoing exercise looking at eighteenth century Manx merchants.

Some information could not be obtained before the book was finished. The du Bois CDROM has not been published yet – it is hoped that this will provide some of the missing information. The Earle letter-book was unavailable for study because it was being rebound, and the work on the Dalemain archive has barely begun.

This book will be launched at a seminar on *Manx Slave Traders* to be held at the Manx Museum in Douglas during September 1999. The purpose of this seminar is to bring together all the people who were contacted during research for the book. This will be an opportunity for them to share their expertise and so enhance our understanding of the Isle of Man's involvement in the Atlantic Slave Trade.

Appendix 1: Manx Slave Traders: Calendar of Events

This Appendix gives a cross-section of the events affecting the Manx Slave Traders between 1700, when the *Blessing* sailed from Liverpool to Africa and 1829, when Hugh Crow died. They are all described in more detail elsewhere

1700   October: Liverpool: the *Blessing*, Thomas Brownbell captain and John Murray supercargo sailed for the Guinea coast

1702   Robert Murrey died on a 'Guinea voyage' (about 12 years before 1714)

1706   20 March: Coast of Guinea: John Christian died

1707   7 July: Barbados: Robert Curlet died,
        leaving 'certain effects in hands of John Murray of Liverpool, merchant'

1715   14 April: Coast of Guinea: Robert Joyner junior died

1718   25 August: Ramsey: Robert Moore & John Murray landed Guinea goods
        25 August: Ramsey: *Peace Galley, Success Galley & Scipio* collected these goods

1719   13 August: Douglas: John Murray imported Guinea goods for Mr Tarleton & Co.
        31 August: Douglas: *Stannage*, John Seacome captain loaded goods for the Maderas
        Guinea voyage: John Kewley died on board *Standish* galley of Liverpool

1720   1 February: Douglas: *Betty* of Dublin, Pat Coody captain, loaded goods for Lisbon
        6 December: Douglas: First importation of Guinea goods by Andrew Savage

1721   3 January: Douglas: *John* sloop, Robert Steward master, collected 7 boxes and 3 trunks of silks and India stuffs for Guernsey
        4 December: Douglas: *Betty*, John James master, took frize, Hewersden cloth and linen cloth to the Maderas

1723   Coast of Guinea: Archibald Holmes died

1724   September: Douglas: Robert Moore, merchant, died

1729   21 February: Douglas: John Williamson loaded goods on board the *John & Elizabeth*, Thomas Whitesides master, for the Maderas
        9 September: Derbyhaven: Thomas Bennett, master of the *Hannah*, loaded potatoes for the Maderas

1731   26 May: Douglas: *Mary*, Michael Chivers loaded goods for Bilbao
        31 May: Douglas: *Margaret*, Patrick Murphey master collected a varied cargo, including 2 trunks. 3 portmanteaux & 8 bales of India goods for Bilbao

1732   1 June: Derbyhaven: *Michael*, William Simnot master, collected 1 trunk & 9 bales of India goods for Bordeaux

1737	13 January: Douglas: Pat Savage's duty owed calculation gives values of individual Guinea goods
	29 March: Douglas: first record of William Murray senior importing Guinea goods. His partnership with cousin John Murray dissolved this year
1738	July: Douglas: Robert Reeves, merchant, died. His business was taken over by his widow, Mary
1740	Isaacar Williamson importing 'several cases, trunks & boxes of India goods – over £9,000 this year alone
1741	October: Douglas: John Murray, merchant, died
	20 November: Douglas: *St George* Guineaman, John Buchan captain, landed rum for William Murray from Barbados
1742	17 February: Derbyhaven: Abel Anderson imported on the *Notre Dame*, William Anderson master, goods valued at over £11,800
	Coast of Guinea: William Stephan died
1744	16 July: Douglas: Peter Arthura imported on the *St Michell*, himself master, goods valued at over £2,150
1745	18 July: Douglas: First record of Paul Bridson importing Guinea goods
	Coast of Guinea: William Kneen died on board *Mercury*, William Bacon captain
1746	March: Douglas: Mary Reeves died. Robert & William took over the business.
	Coast of Guinea: *Postilion* of Liverpool, Thomas Marsden, lost with John Curghey & John Moore on board.
1747	November: Isle of Man: *New Foster* Guineaman, Chris Boutson captain, wrecked
	Coast of Africa: James Waterson junior died
1749	6 June: Douglas: *Jolly Batchelor* of Lancaster Guineaman, Edward Freeman captain, landed rum
1750	June: Ramsey: attempt by George Dow of the Sincerity revenue cruiser to seize Hope dogger with East India goods on board for Thomas Arthur
	September: Coast of Guinea: *New Grace* of Liverpool, Richard Harrison, lost - David Christian & John Cottier on board
	18 December: Sierra Leone: Edward Lawson ordinary seaman on board the *Duke of Argyle*, John Newton captain died
1751	20 January: Sierra Leone: John Bridson, chief mate on the *Duke of Argyle*, John Newton captain, died of a fever
	29 March: Sierra Leone: Thomas Bridson, apprentice on the *Duke of Argyle*, died of a fever
	August: Isle of Man: *Alice* Guineaman, Richard Jackson, wrecked
1752	Coast of Africa: Charles Shimmin died on *Merton* snow of Glasgow, John Coppell captain

1753   July: Douglas: Davenport vessel *Charming Nancy*, Samuel Sacheverell, to collect goods from William Teare
Coast of Guinea: Daniel Cottiman, cooper, died on the *Salisbury*, Thomas Marsden captain

1754   August: Douglas: *Charming Nancy*, Samuel Sacheverell & *James*, Isaac Hyde to collect goods from William Teare

1755   Benin, coast of Africa: Richard Quirk died on *Prince Eugene*, Thomas Kewley captain

1756   January & February: Liverpool: *Chesterfield, Little Dicky, Phoebe & Tom* all cleared from Liverpool with protections from impressment naming Isle of Man and Africa
August: Douglas: William Murray senior died. William Teare executor
August: Douglas: *Nancy*, Thomas Dickson captain, to collect goods from Hugh Cosnahan.

1757:   24 October: Douglas: Philip & George Moore write to Duke of Atholl opposing Thomas Heywood's proposal to build a bridge across the harbour
3 December: Douglas: Captains of 4 Guinea vessels sign statement about the harbour
Abraham Vianna partner in the *Vianna* Guineaman – for one voyage

1758   January: Douglas: *Dahomey*, Tim Nichols captain, ashore and bulged

1759   April: in Irish Sea: seizure of *Isabel*, William Dugdale, from Scotland to Rotterdam and the Isle of Man carrying 600 barrels of gunpowder by Captain Colin Campbell of the *Prince George* revenue cruiser. John Tarleton asked the Duke of Atholl to intervene so that the vessel would be released. Duke took no action. Vessel released and carried gunpowder to Douglas – landed by Paul Bridson

1760   6 June: Liverpool: engagement announced of William Boats to Elizabeth Bridson, daughter of Paul Bridson of Douglas
September: John Black, father of Robert Black of Ross, Black & Christian visited and commented on Douglas.

1761   16 January: *Dove*, Hugh Williams captain, *Prince William*, Philip Kewley & *Young James*, Robert Mitchell, all reported as being 'at the Isle of Man'
7 February: Liverpool: *Tyrrell*, William Hindle captain, to collect goods from John Joseph Bacon & Paul Bridson
22 May: Liverpool: *Chesterfield*, William Earle captain, to take on board goods from Paul Bridson in Douglas
July: Thomas Kewley, commander of the Prince Eugene died of wounds 'he received in an engagement with a French privateer'
September: Douglas Bay: *Wolfe* Guineaman, William Campbell captain, ashore
Coast of Africa: John Cottiman, mariner on the *Recovery*, Chris Berrill captain, died

1762   May: Liverpool: Ambrose Lace's letter of instruction as commander of the *Marquis of Granby* to sail with Michael Finch of the *Douglas* 'who has some business at the Isle of Man'
30 July: Middle Passage: William Kelly died

1763   May, June & July: Liverpool: seizure of the *Henrietta Maria*, Henrick Bremer master, *Marquis de Bonac*, Jan Wolfers and *John*, Hans Neilson by Arthur Onslow

1764   July: Douglas: William Teare died
                20 November: Douglas: *Richmond* Guineaman, Alex Lennox, bulged on pier
                25 November: Liverpool: *William*, William Patten, to collect goods from Hugh Cosnahan.

1765   1 June: London: Revestment Act ended Isle of Man's role as a warehouse for Guinea goods: the trade of the Isle of Man with Great Britain placed under stringent regulation (5 Geo III cap 39).
                Hugh Crow born at Ramsey

1766   Guinea coast: *Rainbow*, William Gill captain, blew up
1766   Casey River, Sierra Leone: John Callister, crew on *Sarah* brig, Joseph Ward captain, drowned
                Liverpool: Atherton & Earle, merchants, allowed to import 19,964 gallons brandy from the Isle of Man 'for shipment 'in the African trade only'

1767   *Edgar*, Ambrose Lace captain, at Old Calabar during the Massacre

1768   Coast of Guinea: Quayle Wattleworth died

1769   November: Matthew Craine died on board the *Lily*, James Salcraig captain
                Voyage of the *Bridson*, John Platt & Lancelot Bird masters. Paul Bridson co-owner

1770   Coast of Guinea: John Geneste died

1771   October: Douglas: Paul Bridson died, aged 78

1772   March: Coast of Guinea: Thomas Harper died on board *Patsey*, Captain Peterson
                26 September: Liverpool: 'This is to certify whom it may concern that John Tear proceeded in the ship *Rose* of Liverpool, James Welsh master, on her last voyage to Africa and that he was overset in said ship's boat going over Junk Bar October 16th 1771 and was drowned'. Signed James Welsh

1775   25 May: 'Died a few days ago at Douglas in the Isle of Man, Captain Michael Finch, many years in the Guinea trade from Liverpool' Cumberland Packet

1776   19 August: Coast of Guinea: Philip Cooper died on board the *Hope*, Captain Fletcher

1779   March: French gaol: John Christory died

1784   12 January: Coast of Guinea: Clive Fargher died on board the *Antigallican*, William Parke captain

1787   Peel: Sir George Moore died.
                14 November: Middle Passage: William Mylrae died

1789   February: Liverpool: the *Ranger*, John Corran captain, sailed

1790   Hugh Crow's first African voyage, as chief mate of the *Prince*

1791   24 February: Coast of Africa: Ross Christian captain of the *Will* died

1792	6 May: Coast of Guinea: Daniel Cubbon died
1792	August: Douglas: Philip Finch, merchant, died
1793	Africa: Thomas Stowell, captain of the *Colonel*, died
1794	June: Kingston, Jamaica: Charles Caine, chief mate on board *Bridget* Guineaman of Liverpool died 16 September: Quimper gaol, France: Alexander Matthews died October: French gaol: Thomas Kelly died
1796	January: Kingston, Jamaica: Henry Lord, chief mate on board the *Dispatch* Guineaman died
1798	24 July: Coast of Guinea: John Corran, captain of the *Triton*, died Hugh Crow's first command of a slave ship: the *Will* belonging to William Aspinall
1799	20 February: Liverpool: Charles Christian sailed as surgeon on board the *William*, Richard Hart captain 23 September: Atlantic Ocean: Hugh Kissack, captain of the *Penny*, drowned 23 September: Robert Waterson, carpenter's mate on the *Penny*, drowned
1800	13 January: Coast of Guinea: Thomas Radcliffe died on board the *Charlotte*, William Crow captain 3 February 1800: Coast of Guinea: William Crow, Hugh Crow's brother & captain of the *Charlotte*, drowned. William Kneal, captain of the *Dart*, died. William Corran, captain of the *Nanny*, died at sea
1802	January: Middle Passage: James Cornish died Coast of Africa: James Gill died
1803	10 May: Surinam: Robert Patton, surgeon on the *Dick*, died Coast of Guinea: Christopher Callow died on board the *Tamar*, Captain May
1804	February: Coast of Africa: Robert Redfern died on board the *Prescot*, Captain Gardener April: Liverpool: Phillip Garrett sailed as surgeon on the *Ceres*, Adam Elliott
1807	July: Liverpool: *Kitty's Amelia*, Hugh Crow captain, sailed
1810	Rushen: Captain Quayle Fargher of Snugborough, died aged 55
1812	Patrick: Captain Charles Kneal of Ragged Farm died
1817	London: John Bean Hannay in Newgate prison awaiting transportation on a charge of slave trading
1829	Captain Hugh Crow died at Crowville(a)

Appendix 2: Guinea Vessels calling at the Isle of Man

This Appendix lists vessels identified as calling at the Isle of Man between 1718 and 1764.

The main sources of information are:

- the Liverpool Trade & Shipping database

- the Manx customs records

- the Liverpool Port Books

- George Moore's correspondence, and

- the Atholl papers

1. Vessels collecting goods for 'the Maderas'

4 April 1721	*Oak*, Christopher Bridson
4 December 1721	*Betty*, John James
13 February 1729	*John & Elizabeth*, Thomas Whitesides
14 April 1729	*John*, Samuel Wallace
September 1729	*Hannah*, Thomas Bennett

2. Vessels collecting Guinea goods in 1718 and 1719

25 August 1718	*Peace Galley*, Cheatwood Pride – owner Foster Cunliffe of Liverpool
	Scipio, Captain Trafford - owner Robert Gildart
	Success Galley, Thomas Moister
	– possibly *Tarleton*, Thomas Tarleton owner
8 September 1718	*Owners Adventure*, possibly Robert Armitage captain & co-owner
9 September 1719	*Stannage*, John Seacombe

3. Vessels collecting gunpowder

a. According to John Tarleton, six Liverpool vessels were due to collect gunpowder which was to have been landed on the Island by the *Isabel*, Walter Dugdale master, from Rotterdam. The following is a list is of possible vessels in this category, all of which appear to have been preparing to sail in April 1759. The *Blackburne* was owned by Tarleton:

Ferret, John Bury
Lyme, John Hoggan
Spy, William Creevey
Isaac, David Clatworthy
Blackburne, Jacob Chambers
Beaver, William Hayes

3. Vessels collecting gunpowder contd.

b. Vessel on which 10 barrels <u>were</u> shipped by Paul Bridson
4 April 1759   *Ann*, Daniel Hayes

4.   Vessels landing goods at the Island from either the West Indies or America

11 November 1741	*St George*, John Buchan
9 September 1745	*Worcester*, William Harrison
6 June 1749	*Jolly Batchelor*, Edward Freeman
19 June 1749	*Molly*, Phil Styth
10 February 1752	*Betty*, Samuel Sacheverell
11 March 1752	*Thomas*, Patrick Allen
7 September 1753	*Nancy*, John Watson
15 October 1755	*Ferrett*, Thomas Whitehead
2 August 1756	*Thomas*, Daniel Hayes
4 August 1756	*Swallow*, William Oard
6 May 1757	*Lowther*, John Houseman
24 July 1758	*Expedition*, Duncan Campbell
26 August 1758	*Sally*, John Thompson
12 January 1759	*Vianna*, William Hutton
24 October 1759	*Lively*, John Giball
5 October 1761	*Young James*, Robert Mitchell
27 April 1762	*Prince Vada*, John Clifton
25 October 1762	*Prince George*, Daniel Baynes
26 November 1762	*Marquis of Granby*, Robert Dodson

5.   Vessels with instructions to collect goods at the Isle of Man

a. Davenport & Co Vessels

26 July 1753	*Charming Nancy*, Samuel Sacheverell - William Teare, Douglas
20 August 1754	*Charming Nancy*, Samuel Sacheverell - William Teare, Douglas
20 August 1754	*James*, Isaac Hyde - William Teare, Douglas
1762	*Plumper*, Richard Dobb – charges mentioned in accounts
7 February 1761	*Tyrell*, William Hindle - John Joseph Bacon, Douglas
25 November 1764	*William*, William Patten - Hugh Cosnahan, Douglas

b. William Boats & Co Vessel
30 May 1762   *Douglas*, Michael Finch

c. William Earle & Co Vessel
22 May 1751   *Chesterfield*, William Earle – Paul Bridson, Douglas

6.   Vessels returning Guinea goods either damaged or surplus to requirements

24 February 1741	*Thomas*, Evan Jones, from Virginia
29 October 1751	*Thomas*, Pat Allen, from Barbados
23 September 1753	*James*, William Sacheverell, from Barbados
14 September 1754	*Rainbow*, Robert Makin, from Barbados

6. Vessels returning Guinea goods either damaged or surplus to requirements contd.

16 August 1755	*Ryder*, John Sacheverell, from Africa
3 May 1756	*Charming Nancy*, Thomas Dickson, from Cork
28 December 1759	*Rebecca*, Robert Boyd, from Africa

7. John Black's Guinea 'Liverpoolians'

When John Black was in Douglas in September 1760 he described the harbour as being thronged with shipping, including Guinea Liverpoolians. The following is a list of Guinea vessels which sailed from Liverpool between 1 September and 3 October 1760. It is possible that they called at Douglas:

> *Beaver*, William Heyes
> *Dove*, Hugh Williams
> *John*, Nicholas Boulton
> *Knight*, William Jenkinson
> *Minerva*, John Farrar
> *Phebe*, John Paul Freeman
> *William & Edward*, William Foster
> *Young James*, Robert Mitchell

8. Vessels reported as being 'at the Isle of Man'

20 February 1753	*Orrell*, James Bennett
16 January 1761	*Dove*, Hugh Williams
16 January 1761	*Knight*, William Jenkinson
16 January 1761	*Prince William*, Philip Kewley

9. Vessels Wrecked on the Island

23 August 1751	*Alice*, Richard Jackson
18 September 1761	*Wolfe*, William Campbell
	New Foster, Chris Boutson

10. Vessels ashore at the Isle of Man

January 1758	*Dahomey*, Timothy Nichols

Note: Bulged at Douglas & goods returned to Liverpool on 'Douglas Packet'

27 October 1758	*Industry*, John Banks

11. Vessels clearing out with Guinea goods

a. 'for Bilbao'

9 July 1729	*Orange Tree*, Thomas Geykin
5 July 1731	*Margaret*, Patrick Murphey
21 July 1731	*Mary*, Michael Chivers

11. Vessels clearing out with Guinea goods contd

b. 'for Lisbon'
1 February 1720   *Betty* of Dublin, Pat Coody
13 November 1721   *John*, Nicholas Hayes

c. 'for Bordeaux'
1 June 1732   *Michael*, William Simnot

d. 'for Guernsey'
17 June 1720   *Thomas*, John Toole
3 January 1721   *John*, Robert Steward

12. Vessels whose Captains signed a statement about Douglas harbour, 1757

Betty, Robert Boyd
Judith, William Heyes
Shaw Perfect, James Carruthers
Minerva of Lancaster, *John Preston*

13. Vessels 'riding in this bay' (Peel), 1758

On 5 January 1758 George Moore wrote to Haliday & Dunbar in Liverpool that there were three Liverpool vessels sheltering in Peel Bay. The following vessels sailed between 30 December 1757 and 6 January 1758 and it is <u>possible</u> that they are the ones referred to by Moore:
Whydah, Chris Ewings
Royal Family, Wilson Shepherd
Prince Tom, Charles Cooke

14. Vessels sheltering at Peel instead of collecting goods at Douglas, 1759

March 1759   *Upton*, John Birch
April 1759   *Hare*, George Colley

15. Vessels with Protections (against impressment) naming the Isle of Man, 1756

20 January 1756   *Tom*, Thomas Hughes
28 January 1756   *Chesterfield*, Patrick Black
1 February 1756   *Little Dicky*, George Miller
1 February 1756   *Phoebe*, James Bennet

Appendix 3: East Indian Cloths and Guinea Goods

This Appendix shows the range of East Indian cloths and Guinea goods available on the Island for collection by slaving vessels.

1. East Indian cloths imported into the Isle of Man between 1718 and 1764

addilies, alhibanees [allibanes], allegars [allejars], annabasses

bafts [shalbafts], ballasous, bandanoes, bejulapants, birampants [byrampants], Bombay stuffs, brawls

calico, cardonnees, carridarries, catterees, chalioncas, chanderbanies, charconnees [cherconnees], checkaloes [chuckaloes], chelloes [chilloes/aes], chintz, chollocs [chocalees], cholloys, chucanees, cossars, cottons, culgees, cushtoes, cuttaness

dimitty, duconas, fustian, gamwars [jamwars], ginghams grogoroons [grogroons, grograms], Guinea cloth

hammans, hannoes, herbas, humhums

lamopasses [lampass, lempasses], lawns, lemanees [lemmanees, lemonees], long cloth, longees [lungees]

morees, mungae mungae, muslin, nankeens, negannepants, negrapants, nellaes [nillaes], niccanees [niconnees]

padusoys, painted cottons, palempores, patnas, pelongs, pemasiolas, peniascoes, persians, photaes, poisees [pooseys, poysees], polongs [poolongs]

romals, salempores [selempores], seckersoys, seecunes, seersuckers, sepoys, sestracundes, silks, sooseys

taffadofoolas, taffetas, tape, tapseils, topays, tupoises, velare and velvet

2. Descriptions of some of these East Indian cloths
Note: These descriptions come from both the customs entries themselves and from published sources

annabasses: cotton stuff aka fustian
baft: coarse white cotton cloth
brawl: blue and white striped cloth – used as turbans
chillae: poor quality checked or striped cotton cloth
gingham: striped or checked cotton
Guinea cloth: plain, checked or striped cotton
longee: plain cotton cloth - sometimes described as herba (silk)
muslin: fine cotton cloth
nillae: striped or plain cotton
painted cotton: with floral, geometric or figurative decorations
palempore: cotton with printed or painted decorations - a flowering tree or large-scale floral design
patna: inexpensive cloth made of cotton and silk mix
romal: cotton or silk square used as neckerchief. Colours mentioned: red, white & blue
salempore: plain, dyed (usually blue) cotton cloth in a range of qualities
tape: inexpensive painted cottons
other cottons: niccannees, photaes and tapseil

3. *Morgenstar*, **William Christian master, at Douglas from Rotterdam in September 1760**
Note: This is the only Dutch vessel at Douglas during John Black's visit (see Table 3.1)

2 bales of bafts, 18 chests and 2 boxes of beads and 48 cases of beads and looking glasses with a total value of £1,130 plus 2,300 iron bars and 2 casks and 1 case containing 354 dozen knives, all for the Guinea trade. The merchants entering the Guinea goods were Paul Bridson, Hugh Cosnahan and John Finch. The cargo also included geneva, tea, tobacco and writing paper The tea was valued at £417.

3.   The *Vrede* & the *Marquis de Bonac*, Jan Wolfers master:
Summary of goods brought to Douglas from Rotterdam between 1750 and 1763

Arrangoes: 1 box & 1 case; beads: 8 casks, 48 chests, 2 cases & 2 boxes; beads & hawk bells: 13 casks; beads & cowries: 5 chests, 31 casks & cases & 1 box; corals: 4 cases; French horns: 1 case; looking glasses: 1 case & 1 box; trumpets & flutes: 1 cask
Bafts: 28 bales & 3 casks; blue bafts: 8 chests; bafts & arrangoes: 2 bales & 1 case; bafts & hang bells: 2 casks: bafts, photaes, romals & selempores: 7 casks; bandannas & handkerchiefs: 140 pieces; calicoes & lawns: 1 chest; chintz: 1 case & 10 pieces; chintz, silesias, lay cloths & knittings: 3 chests; cotton chelloes: 3 bales; cotton covers: 1 box; cotton romals: 14 bales & 6 chests; cotton romals, chintz & photaes: 3 casks; Dresden ruffles: 12 pieces; India cottons: 2 bales & 100 pieces; old sheets: more than 1 chest & 2 cases; patnas: 1 chest; photaes: 1 cask & 107 pieces; photaes & selempores: 1 cask; sestracundes: 4 chests & 2 cases; silesias: 4 chests; silks: 1 pipe & 1 case; woollen stuffs: 5 bales
Cowries: 277 casks & 50 cases; spread eagle dollars: more than 7 bags
Brass & copper rods: more than one case; brass pans: 5 casks & 1 case; Guinea pans: 1 cask; neptunes: 21 casks
China: 1 case; empty guardvins: over 40; Hungary water: 1 case
Gunflints: 12,000
Ling fish: 48 bundles & 14 hoops; ling & stock fish: 40 bundles; stockfish: 330 bundles 117 hoops and 5 hundredweight

5. Guinea goods landed at Douglas by the *Henrietta Maria*, Henrick Bremer master
Note: This vessel was seized when she arrived at Liverpool on 5 May 1763

Merchants: Paul Bridson; Christian Brown; William Callow; John Christian; Hugh Connor; Val Connor; Francis Dean; Robert Gordon; Robert Kennedy; Charles Killey; Robert Mercer; William Quayle; Ross, Black & Christian; Stowell & Geneste; John Taubman; William Tear & Robert Whiteside

Goods: Bafts: 5 bales; Beads: 2 cases; Brandy: 12 pieces & 6 puncheons containing 5 tons; Brown paper: 4 bales containing 80 rheams; Cambric: 20 pieces 160 yds; China; Cloves: 1 case & 3 lbs; Combs: 1 doz; Flax: 43 stone; Geneva: 1 piece, 8 pipes, 114 hogsheads, 1 puncheon & 8 guardvins containing 24¼ tons; Iron: 200 bars weighing 2 tons; Juniper berries: 6 chests, 24 bales; Lintseed oil: 1 cask containing 30 galls; Looking glasses: 12 doz; Madder: 8 cwt; Nutmegs: 6 lbs; Old sheets: 1 case; Parchment: 4 sheets; Pepper: 2 casks containing 153½ lbs; Silesias: 1 case; Silks: 1 box; Starch; Sugar candy: 1 bale containing 120½ lbs; Tea: 151 chests & 70 boxes; Vinegar: 1 barrel; Whalebone: 48½ lbs; Wine: 12 ankers containing 120 gallons; Writing paper: 25 rheams plus. of which John Taubman imported 20 chests of tea and 40 hogsheads of geneva.

6. Contents of Trunks of East India goods imported by Hugh Cosnahan

Note: These trunks were landed at Douglas from the *Success*, Charles Lace master, on 26 February 1751.

Containers: 6 trunks and one box of India goods valued at £1007 3s 10d.

Contents: 496 bandannas, 169 pieces of chintz, 137 romals, 60 carridary shirts, 19 ginghams, 17 handkerchiefs, 9 of which were silk, 16 sooseys, 7 chuckaloes, 6 tafettas, 4 seckersoy, 2 painted dimmity, 1 piece each of blue grogram and seersucker and 7 jiltmills.

Appendix 4a: Manx Partnerships in Guinea Vessels: Merchants

Merchant & Vessels	Type	Tonnage	Crew	Guns	Slaves (BT)	Reg Date	No. of Voyages	Notes
John Joseph Bacon								
Prince Vada	Brigantine	100	25	10	250	1760	1	Co-owners: William Quayle & Hugh Cosnahan (see below) & William Davenport, Patrick Black, William Heyes, Robert Jennings & William Earle. Called at Douglas with brown sugar on homeward voyage
Rumbold I	Ship	200	34	4	500	1764	3	Co-owners: Thomas Rumbold, William Snell & Michael Finch. Finch captain for 2 voyages. 3rd voyage, Evan Livesley captain, 1767 lost on bar at Bonny with 390 slaves on board. 28 slaves on board & crew saved
Hare	Ship	150	40	6	400	1769	2	Co-owners: Thomas Rumbold, Thomas Falkner, John Simmons, Michael Finch & Thomas Looney. Looney listed as captain but William Chapman sailed from Liverpool. 2nd voyage buried 186 slaves at Grenada. Lost at sea on homeward voyage, leaky after a gale. Crew safe.
Rumbold II	Ship	200	35	8	480/460 450	1769	6	Co-owners: Thomas Rumbold, John Simmons & Michael Finch. Finch captain for 3 voyages. 1st outward voyage put into Ramsey Bay damaged. 4th voyage captain, John Thompson, died in Middle Passage – 1773
Venus	Ship	200	34	8		1772	2	Co-owners: Thomas Rumbold, William Dennison, John Simmons & Michael Finch
Paul Bridson								
Sisters	Brigantine	70	20	4	160	1768	1	Co-owners: John Cope, William Morris, Henry Kirkby & John Wright
Bridson	Snow	80	20	8	160	1769	1	Co-owners: Richard Hanley, John Johnson, Edward Bridge, Daniel Jones, John Fisher, Roger Fisher, John Platt & Walter Cahoun

Merchant & Vessels	Type	Tonnage	Crew	Guns	Slaves (BT)	Reg Date	No. of Voyages	Notes
Hugh Cosnahan *Prince Vada*								see John Joseph Bacon
Douglas	Ship	200	60	20	500	1762	1	Co-owners: James Oates, John Maine, William Stewart, Robert Green, Daniel Jones, Thomas Smith, James Campbell & Michael Finch. Finch captain. Called at Isle of Man and landed cheese
John Finch *Bacchus*	Snow	80	26/30	4	200/250	1773	2	Co-owners: William Earle, Nehemiah Holland, William Dennison, Thomas Hodgson jnr, George Warren Watts & Thomas Earle 1777 - taken by a privateer on the Middle Passage, John Forsyth captain
Robert Gordon *Four Friends*	Sloop	20	10	10	53	1760	0	Co-owners: John Dawson, Thomas Dawson & John Montgomery Originally named *Charming Molly*. Renamed but apparently did not sail from Liverpool
Robert Kennedy *Molly*	Ship	100	35	12/14	300	1760	2	1st voyage (1761) reported from Jamaica that had buried 107 slaves
Warree	Snow	80	10	6	160	1762	1	Ready but did not sail on 2nd voyage
Nancy I	Ship	100	16	4	300	1763	1	According to Lloyds List arrived at St Kitts from Old Calabar with 230 slaves on 5 March 1765
Nancy II	Ship	100	30	4	350	1766	1	Same vessel as above but rebuilt at Liverpool 1766
Favourite	Brigantine	70	20	4	200/150	1767	2	In 1769 at Kissey River the local natives freed 96 slaves and seized the cargo. The ship and crew were freed and sailed to Liverpool, where the goods were imported.

119

Merchant & Vessels	Type	Tonnage	Crew	Guns	Slaves (BT)	Reg Date	No. of Voyages	Notes
Robert Kennedy contd.								
Lord Cassils I	Snow	80	30	6	300	1767	1	According to Lloyds List arrived at Antigua from Kissey river with 220 slaves on 3 January 1769
Ann	Ship	100	37	6	350	1768	1	Michael Finch co-owner.
Lord Cassils II	Snow	80	35	6	260	1769	1	Same vessel as above but re-registered. According to Lloyds List at Barbados from the Windward Coast with 219 slaves on 24 April 1770
Ann	Ship	100	37/30	6	400	1770	2	On homeward voyage from Barbados in March & April 1771 put into Crook in Ireland & Beaumaris in Wales. Her goods were imported into Liverpool on 19 April
Carrick	Schooner	30	12	4/6	120/80	1770	2	William Bickerstaff, who was appointed captain for both voyages killed on the coast of Africa in July 1771. Vessel brought home by Peter Fenton
Lord Cassils III	Ship	80	40/35	14/10	400/350	1771	2	Previous *Lord Cassils*, now a ship. Captain Henry Madden died at Old Calabar on 1 November 1771 and the vessel was brought home by Samuel McCutchen. John Sime was captain on the second voyage
May	Brigantine	70	15	4	250	1771	1	Lost at Cape Verde on outward voyage. Crew taken to Antigua
Industry	Brigantine	70	21	4	160	1772	1	Both voyages to Old Calabar. Advertised for sale: apply Robert Kennedy at Liverpool
May	Brigantine	70	20	10/6	250	1772	2	2nd voyage was from Ayr to Gibraltar & Malaga and back to Liverpool
Carrick	Brigantine	30	12	6	80	1772	1	
Thomas	Ship	100	24	5	250	1772	1	William Davenport co-owner. Recaptured the *Matty*, Samuel Pemberton, which had been cut off by natives in October and the crew killed. Benjamin Burrows brought her home. She was re-registered the *King George* in 1793 – a Davenport/Earle/Ambrose Lace vessel

120

Merchant & Vessels	Type	Tonnage	Crew	Guns	Slaves (BT)	Reg Date	No. of Voyages	Notes
Robert Kennedy contd. *Robert*	Snow	80	28	6	250	1772	1	In 1774 ran ashore near Milford on homeward voyage from Jamaica. Sank in deep water. The *Providence* imported the goods from the wreck.
James Oates *Douglas*								see Hugh Cosnahan above
William Quayle *Prince Vada*								see John Joseph Bacon above
Abraham Vianna *Vianna*	Snow	80	24	4	250	1757	1	Co-owners: Charles Ford, James Gildart, William Higginson, Barth Sherlock, Samuel Winstanley & Thomas Wycliffe. Put into Belfast on homeward voyage

Notes

i.   Based on the Liverpool Trade & Shipping database
ii. Slaves (BT) refers to the number of slaves according to the Board of Transport papers. It does not mean that this number of slaves was either collected on the African coast or sold in the West Indies etc
iii. 480/460 etc refers to different numbers on different voyages
iv. Reg date refers to date of Liverpool Plantation register
v.   I, II etc for current reference purposes only
vi. 0 voyages means that the vessel prepared for a voyage but did not sail. The *Dolphin* has not been included here (see Chapter 7)
vii. information about Robert Kennedy's partnerships is listed in Table 7.1

121

Appendix 4b: Manx Partnerships in Guinea Vessels: Captains

Captain & Vessels	Type	Tonnage	Crew	Guns	Slaves (BT)	Reg Date	No. of Voyages	Notes
Michael Finch								
Charming Fanny	Ship	200	60	20	500	1760	1	Co-owners: John Maine, Robert Green, William Stuart & James Coates
Douglas								See 4a. above
Rumbold I & II								See 4a. above. Finch captain for 4 voyages
Henry Frissell								
Mersey	Snow	80	30	6	200	1752	0	Co-owners: Peter Holmes, John Kennion & Henry Widdens
Juno	Snow	90	25	12	300	1752	1	Co-owners: Peter Holmes & John Kennion. 2 voyages. 2nd Guinea coast – Frissel captain for this one.
William Gill								
Tyrell	Ship	85	40	14	400	1759	1	Co-owners: John Maine, Robert Green, William Sandford & William Stewart. Taken by *Byn* privateer into St Jean de Luz [France] on homeward voyage
Meredith	Ship	110	?	?	450	1761	1	Co-owners: John Maine, Roger Haydock, Thomas Hodgson, Jonathan Radcliffe & Thomas Rumbold. Vessel returned from West Indies to London
Cato	Ship	100	35	6	350/ 300/ 400	1767	3	Co-owners: Thomas Rumbold & Michael Finch. 3rd voyage – November 1771 cut off in the Benin river and all the crew killed
William Lawson								
Rose	Ship	200	60/70	18	600	1758	2	Co-owners: John Welch, Edward Parr, Thomas Johnson & George Hulton
								Note: Lawson was also a co-owner of the *Ogden*, Alexander Lawson captain

Captain & Vessels	Type	Tonnage	Crew	Guns	Slaves (BT)	Reg Date	No. of Voyages	Notes
Philip Kewley *Racehorse*	Brigantine	30	20	6	160	1758	2	Co-owners: George Cowper, Daniel Jones, George Mercer, William Reid, John Renshaw & David Winstanley. Referred to by William Davenport as 'Captain Kewley & Co'. Kewley only captain for 1st voyage. 2nd - Taken into Martinique with 120 slaves on board.
Prince William	Ship	161	30	14	300	1760	1	Co-owners: Daniel McNeale & William Reid. 'Captain Kewley & Co' (see above). At Isle of Man on outward voyage.
Peggy	Snow	70	?	?	200	1763	1	John Renshaw & Charles Ford. Lost on Guinea coast
Ambrose Lace *Hector*	Ship	150	34	6	450/400	1765/1769	6	Co-owners: William Crosbie, James Baird, David Bean, Samule Bean, John Crosbie, Lewis Cuthbert, William Rowe, James Simson & William Trafford. Lace appears to have taken over as captain on 1st voyage at Grenada. 2 voyages in Davenport accounts. 3rd voyage buried 20 slaves at Dominica. 5th voyage Captain Doyle poisoned by natives on African coast – arrived at Grenada with slaves in bad condition. 6th voyage ran aground on Hoy Bank – considerable damage. Sailed 3 weeks later. In collision with HMS *Seaford* in West Indies & condemned.
Edgar	Ship	150	40	8	2	1767	2	Co-owners: John Bailey, Edward Chaffers, John Crosbie, William Crosbie, Robert Green, William Rowe, William Trafford. Lace was captain on 1st voyage – massacre at Old Calabar. Henry Madden captain on 2nd voyage – slaves sold at South Carolina

Captain & Vessels	Type	Tonnage	Crew	Guns	Slaves (BT)	Reg Date	No. of Voyages	Notes
Thomas Looney								
Brothers	Snow	120	28	6	300	1766	1	Co-owners: John Brown, William Levington & John McAllister
Brothers	Snow	100	27	6	300	1767	1	Co-owners: as above
Hare								See 4a. above – John Joseph Bacon
Henry Moore								
Blayds	Ship	200	60/50	24/6	(400)	1782	2	Co-owners: Chris Butler, Peter Baker, John Cleminson, John Dawson, Francis Ingram, John Kaye, & David Tuohy
Robert Waterson								
Essex	Snow	100	25	8/6	250	1759	9	Co-owners: Thomas Johnson, James Brown, William Dobb, Thomas Foxcroft, John Goad, George Hutton & John Salthouses. Waterson captain for first 3 voyages.

Notes

i.   Based on the Liverpool Trade & Shipping database

ii.   Slaves (BT) refers to the number of slaves according to the Board of Transport papers. It does not mean that this number of slaves was either collected on the African coast or sold in the West Indies etc. ( ) indicates not a BT source

iii. 480/460 etc refers to different numbers on different voyages

iv.   Reg date refers to date of Liverpool Plantation register

v.   *I, II* etc for current reference purposes only

vi.   0 voyages means that the vessel prepared for a voyage but did not sail.

vii. There is further information about Ambrose Lace and Michael Finch in Chapter 7. Table 7.2 lists Lace's vessels once he was a Liverpool merchant

Appendix 5: Manx Mariners who died 'on the Guinea coast'

Note: This list is not intended to be exhaustive as new information becomes available constantly.

Name	Vessel	Captain	When	Parish	Source
John Allan	*King of Prussia*	Samuel Richardson	31 December 1769	Maughold	GL716
James Black			about 1770	Rushen	GL717
John Bridson	*Duke of Argyle*	John Newton	20 January 1751		JNJ
Thomas Bridson	*Duke of Argyle*	John Newton	29 March 1751		JNJ
Thomas Brideson			between 1783 & 1790	Castletown	GL725
Patrick Caley	*Mars*	Captain Wade	before August 1789	German	GL724
John Callister	*Sarah Brig*	Joseph Ward	January 1766	Braddan & Douglas	GL714
Christopher Callow	*Tamar*	Captain May	August 1803	Maughold	GL730
Thomas Cannell	*Neptune*	James Williams	before September 1799	Arbory	GL728
Thomas Cannon	*Bleak (Admiral Blake)*	Alex Talbot	June 1750/51	Michael	GL709
David Christian			about 1750	Braddan & Douglas	GL711
David Christian	*Parr*	himself	1798		HC
John Christian			20 March 1706	Onchan	EW30
Ross Christian	*Will*	himself	24 February 1791		MR
William Clucas			1785/1786	Arbory	GL723
Philip Cooper	*Hope*	Captain Fletcher	19 August 1776	Peel	GL719
Thomas Corkan	*Ryder*	Michael Rush	about 1752	German	GL709
Robert Corlett			October 1751	Ballaugh	GL709

Name	Vessel	Captain	When	Parish	Source
John Corran	*Triton*	himself	24 July 1798		MR
Daniel Cotteman	*Salisbury*	Thomas Mastone	about February 1753	Ballaugh	GL709
James Cottier	*New Grace*		September 1750	German	GL709
John Cottiman	*Recovery*	John Barrell	some time before 1761	Onchan	GL712
Thomas Cowley	*Lion* of London		'some time ago' in 1793	Ramsey	GL726
Hugh Cowlle			1803		GL732
Mathew Craine	*Lilly*	James Salcraig	November 1769	Lonan	GL716
Patrick Craine	*Renown*	Captain Pickering	February 1760		GL715
Henry Creer			about 1759	Braddan & Douglas	GL713
William Crow	*Charlotte*	himself	3 February 1800	Ramsey	GL729/ MR
Daniel Cubbon			6 May 1792	Marown	GL725
John Curghey			about 1746	Lezayre	GL709
Clive Fargher	*Antigallican*	William Parke	12 July 1784		GL721
John Garrett			about October 1792	Ramsey	GL726
John Geneste			1770	Malew	GL719
James Gill			1802	Lezayre	GL730
Thomas Harper	*Patsey*	Captain Peterson	March 1772	Malew	GL716
Richard Harrison	*Royal African*		about October 1750	Marown	GL709
Walker Hoare			between 1739 & 1743	Castletown & Malew	GL706

Name	Vessel	Captain	When	Parish	Source
Archibald Holmes			about May 1723	Malew	EW32
John Hutchin			about 1718	Castletown	EW32
Robert Joyner	*Little Foster*	Captain Cropper	1752?	Braddan & Douglas	GL709
Robert Joyner jnr			14 April 1715	Braddan	EW29
Thomas Kaighin					
John Kelly	*Hope* of London	John Teare	about October 1763	Braddan & Douglas	GL713?
James Kewley			between 1737 & 1739		EW37
John Kewley	*Standish galley*		1719?		
Philip Kinread	*King Edgar*	Henry Madden	Christmas 1769		GL716
Robert Kinvegg			about 1746	Arbory	GL712
William Kneen	*Mercury*	William Bacon	about 1745	Lezayre	GL707
Edward Lawson	*Duke of Argyle*	John Newton	18 December 1750	Andreas	GL715/JNJ
Peter Miller	*Dart*	Edward Crosby	March 1802		MR
John Moore			about 1745	Maughold	GL709
William Moore	*Bolton*	J Boardman	between November 1798 & Novembver 1799	Patrick	GL728
Robert Murrey			about 1704?	Ramsey	GL699
John Quay			May 1760	Onchan	GL713
Richard Quirk	*Prince Eugene*	Thomas Kewley	before December 1755	Patrick	GL711?
Thomas Quirk			about November 1750	Patrick	GL708

Name	Vessel	Captain	When	Parish	Source
William Quirk jnr			about 1745	Patrick	GL708
Thomas Radcliffe	*Charlotte*	William Crow	13 January 1800	Lezayre	GL729/MR
Robert Redfern	*Prescot*	Gardener	February 1804	Malew	GL732
Robert Sayle	*Aurora*		?	Douglas	GL730
William Shimin	*African*		before November 1803	Malew	GL730
Charles Shimmin	*Merton* of Glasgow	John Coppell	8 April 1752	Malew	GL709
William Stephan			about 12 months before July 1743	Jurby	GL706
Thomas Taubman			about 1758	Malew/Arbory	GL719
John Tear	*Rose*	James Welch		Jurby	GL716
James Waterson jnr			1747	Rushen	RB580
Quayle Wattleworth			September 1768	Malew	GL716
Charles White	*Mars*	Captain Wade	before July 1789	German	GL724
Robert Woods			November 1750	Malew	GL709

Key: EW: Episcopal wills microfilm
        GL: Episcopal wills microfilm
        RB: Archdeaconal wills microfilm

        HC: Hugh Crow's Memoirs
        JNJ: John Newton's Journal
        MR: Port of Liverpool Muster Roll

Appendix 6: Ambrose Lace's voyages as Captain of a Slaving Vessel

VOYAGE 1
1754: 28 February	sailed from Liverpool as master of the *Duke of Chester*
1755: 21 February	at Old Calabar
6 May	left Africa for Kingston, Jamaica - 184 slaves on board
4 July	at Jamaica
19 August	cleared out from Kingston for Chester
31 October	ashore in Carnarvon Bay on way from Jamaica to Chester.

VOYAGE 2
1756: 10 September	sailed from Liverpool as master of the *Lintot*
1757: 24 June	at Africa
16 September	passed Barbados
14 October	at South Carolina
16 December	ashore near Crosby bulged, feared most of the cargo lost

VOYAGE 3
1758: 8 September	cleared out at Liverpool as master of the *Marlborough*
22 September	ashore at Crosby Point but got off
23 September	sailed from Liverpool again
1759: 1 January	at Whydah
29 July	cleared from Africa for Charlestown with 293 slaves on board
21 September	at South Carolina
7 December	at Liverpool
21 December	vessel advertised for sale by owners: Crosbies & Trafford

VOYAGE 4
1760: 28 April	sailed from Liverpool as master of the *Marlborough*
1761: 30 January	sailed from Calabar with 300 slaves
20 February	arrived at Antigua with 280 slaves
?	returned to Liverpool. William Benson appointed captain of vessel

VOYAGE 5
1762: 14 April	letter of instruction as master of *Marquis of Granby*[163]
21 June	at Calabar
1763: 11 February	at Martinique with 345 slaves
6 May	returned to Liverpool from Guadeloupe

VOYAGE 6
1763: 5 July	entered out from Liverpool as master of the *Marquis of Granby*
1764: 8 June	entered out from Africa for Kingston with 340 slaves
3 August	at Jamaica
3 September	cleared from Kingston for Liverpool
October	foundered at sea - crew saved. Taken back to West Indies?

VOYAGE 7
| 1766: 18 April | sailed from Grenada as master of the *Hector*[164] |
| 13 May | arrived at Liverpool |

VOYAGE 8
1767: 22 May	sailed from Liverpool as master of the *Edgar*
4 December	at Old Calabar and half slaved
1768: 5 April	at Antigua with 300 slaves
22 April	goods imported at Liverpool

Source Material

This essay describes the different source material which was collected during the research for the book. The material came under specific headings: customs data, vessels, merchants, mariners, the triangular voyage and the slave trade per se.

❖ Customs data was required to prove that Guinea goods were landed on the Isle of Man, that they were collected by Guinea vessels on their way to the coast of west Africa and that the homeward bound Guinea vessels landed rum and other goods on the Island.

Most of this information came from the same source: the customs entries held at the Manx National Heritage library in Douglas. It included both the official books of Ingates, Outgates & Herring Customs which were completed by the comptroller and a copy submitted to the Duke of Atholl – the revenue rolls that George Dow was so interested in seizing at Kirkcudbright - and the individual dockets which the merchants were given to take to the deputy searcher at the port where their goods were to be landed – this system has been described through Thomas Stowell. These dockets were stored at the port.

The Ingates and Outgates books are the best source because they record not only all the entries for all the ports on the Island by date but they also include the duties payable. The books run from the Christmas quarter through to Michaelmas so that for 1747 it is necessary to look at both the 1747 and the 1748 books. It was in these books that the ticks were found (or not found as the case may be) when the 1802 analysis of the East India goods was undertaken (see Chapter 3). Figure 1.1 is from the Ingates for 1718.

The dockets are also classed in quarters but all the quarters for one year are stored together. They do not have details of the actual duties although there is an indication as to whether duty was paid or not paid – see Paul Bridson's entries in Figure 3.2. Also they are filed by Port so that it could be easy to miss an importation that was supposed to have been at Douglas but was in fact at Derbyhaven.

Both the Ingates and the dockets provide the information necessary to prove that goods came to the island. The information about vessels actually calling at the Island was recorded in the Outgates section of the customs books. Possible reasons why these records did not continue through the 1730s have been discussed. An example of the Outgates is shown in Figure 1.2.

This information is so extensive that it had to be computerised. This is one of the datasets to be lodged at the Manx National Heritage library.

Information about the vessels in the outgates was found in the Liverpool Port Books, held at the PRO, Kew. They give details of the goods loaded on Guinea vessels at the Liverpool end of their voyages, before calling at the Isle of Man. Only the Port Books for 1718, 1719, 1721 and 1722 were used in this research.

❖ Vessels

The best source of information about Guinea vessel which had connections with the Isle of Man is the Liverpool Trade & Shipping 1744 to 1786 database. This is an excellent resource and has been used very extensively. In particular it provides information about vessel names, types, ownership, masters and voyages.

This database provided much of the information about the Manx partnerships which formed the basis of Chapter 7.

The other secondary source of information about vessels is the parallel research being undertaken by others in related areas: David Richardson was involved with the Liverpool Trade & Shipping database and his work on Whitehaven and Bristol has also been invaluable to this study. The Lancaster information was supplied by Melinda Elder. Finally Eric Graham has studied the Scottish vessels and their voyages.

❖ Both the merchants based on the Isle of Man and those trading with the Island were of interest.

The ideal merchant record is an individual's letterbooks and accounts. Wills are also an important source, particularly if the merchant who died was heavily in debt. These debt cases and other arguments can be traced through the court records. Finally there are various other primary sources at the Manx National Heritage library which provide a wide range of additional information about merchants and their concerns.

Letter-books – fortunately the letter-books of several eighteenth century merchants have survived, although they do make one wonder about what has been lost. In this context the letters of merchants on the island have been supplemented by merchant records both in England and Scotland. The merchant correspondence found included:

Manx Merchant: George Moore: a microfilm of his letter-book is held at the Manx National Heritage library, where it was studied previously by the author in research for *George Moore & Friends*

Liverpool Merchants:
William Davenport: his records have been studied by other workers, in particular David Richardson. The Davenport accounts and letters for several voyages are held at the University of Keele - they are also available on microfilm. In the present context Davenport is of interest because:
- his captains were instructed to call at the Island Man for part of their Guinea cargoes
- he was co-owner of some of Ambrose Lace's vessels and also co-owner with John Joseph Bacon, Hugh Cosnahan and William Quayle of the *Prince Vada*
- his Waste Book includes notes about several Manx merchants

Christopher Hasell's papers are held at Dalemain. They give an interesting insight into the problems in Liverpool post Revestment when gunpowder and other goods shipped off from the Island flooded the local market (see Chapter 6). A crew list which included Manx mariners was found among is papers. Further research on this source is underway

John Tarleton: his papers are held at the Liverpool Record Office. [There is also correspondence from John Tarleton to the Duke of Atholl in the Atholl papers at Douglas]. Tarleton's links with the Island have been described in Chapters 2 and 3. The comments about Paul Bridson & Philip Moore & Co in the Tarleton accounts are another example of the knock-on effect of Revestment.

The Thomas Leyland papers, held at the Liverpool Record Office, were of particular interest because they include letters of instruction to both Charles Kneal and Caesar Lawson (see below)

William Earle: with the exception of the letter of instruction to William Earle, captain of the *Chesterfield*, these papers were not available for study during the research. A copy of this letter is held at the Manx National Heritage library. It suggests a link between Paul Bridson and the Earles.

The letter-books of a Whitehaven merchant, Walter Lutwidge and an Irvine merchant, Robert Arthur, already transcribed by the author, were searched for Manx references.

Wills

The Manx wills are all on microfilm and are of two types: Archidiaconal and Episcopal. In theory there is 'no difference in the substance or circumstances'. The separation was purely administrative: for six months the wills were considered by one court and for six months by the other. In practice the Episcopal wills provide the more valuable information.

The wills were used in two different ways. The card index was searched for the wills of particular individuals, for example Paul Bridson (yes), Hugh Crow (yes) and Ambrose Lace (no). As a separate exercise each film for the period 1696 to 1820 was searched for individuals clearly involved in the slave trade (see the section on mariners below).

The individuals can be divided into two categories. Those who made wills and those who died intestate. Where wills exist there sometimes several additional papers, including accounts submitted in support of debts claimed. Much of the information about John Murray's partnerships came from this source.

Papers from an individual who died intestate may also provide other information about the slave trade, as evidence had to be given by several people that the person was dead and that he did not leave a will.

Several wills of Manx people connected with the Guinea trade are held elsewhere than on the Island. The Lancashire and Cheshire Record Society have produced an excellent guide to the wills 'now preserved in the probate registry, Chester'. For instance Ambrose Lace's will was located in this way – it is now held at the Lancashire Record Office in Preston. A further 20 wills relating to Manxmen involved in the slave trade were also obtained from this source.

Copies of William Boats's wills and probate, together with other family papers, are held at the Denbighshire record Office – his son, Henry Ellis Boats, died in Denbighshire.

Other papers at the Manx National Heritage Museum

A variety of court records were found useful:

The Chancery Court records provide information about Liverpool merchants' connections on the Island - mainly in the form of unpaid debts. The Exchequer Court and Admiralty Court records (in the Petition Files) add further details.

The Atholl Papers include correspondence that was directed to the Duke of Atholl. The account of George Moore's attempts to prevent the building of Douglas bridge, enlarge Peel harbour and attract the Guinea ships from the east to the west side of the Island given in Chapter 5 is based largely on these papers. There are also general comments from the Governor of the Island about the Guinea trade. In addition letters from the Liverpool merchants, John Tarleton and Thomas Mears were found here (see Chapter 3). And the letter signed by the mayor and Liverpool merchants (see Chapter 5).

The Bridge House papers supplement the George Moore information with his letter-book from 1750 to 1760. The letters from Hugh Cosnahan to George Moore (Chapter 6) are in this collection.

Manx Family History Society
This is an opportunity to pay tribute to the excellent work produced by the Society. Their booklets of Monumental Inscriptions and Burial Registers are an invaluable source of information about merchants and their families.

❖ Manx mariners. Here the information required included the ship captains, the crew and the surgeons on board the Guinea vessels

Muster Rolls
The muster rolls contain 'the names of the officers and seamen that were on board the vessel at her departure from this port, and of such as were shipped aboard, with the times when any, and which of them, died, were killed, drowned, ran away, or were discharged, here or aboard, and the time of the ship's sailing hence'. The Liverpool (and Bristol) muster rolls were first used by the Reverend Edward Clarkson to calculate the mortality rate on Guinea ships. They were also used by Stephen Behrendt in his analysis of slave captains. Here they have allowed confirmation of the names of the vessels with Manx masters.

Several muster rolls have been studied – in particular those that related to a particular voyage: that of the *Ranger*, John Corran captain, the *William*, Charles Christian surgeon and the *Kitty's Amelia*, Hugh Crow's last command.

An analysis of the Manx crews on board the vessels with Manx captains has started – comments are found in Chapters 10, 11 and 12. This is the beginning of a more far-reaching project which will computerise all this information for further analysis.

Other Information
Inevitably wills are also a good source of information when trying to assess the numbers of Manx mariners who died in the Guinea trade. Several of the wills of the Manx captains are held at the Lancashire Record Office (see above).

The Court records at the Manx National Heritage library were also of use here – the Court of Gaol Delivery records provided information about William Kneen and the Ecclesiastical Court heard the petition of Thomas Tear's family (see Chapter 10).

❖ The Triangular Trade. It has been impossible not to quote from the Island's best secondary source about the Guinea trade: Hugh Crow's Memoirs. In particular he has provided information about the triangular trade. It has been possible, however, to supplement this information from other sources:

Instructions to Shipmasters
Sometimes the detailed instructions from the owners of a vessel or partners in a particular voyage have survived. These provide invaluable information about the slave trade - from what type of slaves to purchase on the African coast to where to sell the cargo, and on what terms. Instructions written to Manx shipmasters are found in the Thomas Leyland letter-books at Liverpool Record Office and in Gomer Williams' book.

Other Information
The 'Remarks on board the *Ranger*, John Corran captain', held at the Liverpool Record Office is essentially a log book of the voyage. It has been used to illustrate the everyday life of a crew, the problems with crews on board ship and the slowness of the actual purchasing of slaves on the Guinea coast (see Chapters 8, 10 and 11).

Another insight into the trade from a Manx viewpoint was found in a secondary source – John Newton's Journal (see Chapter 10).

❖ The Slave Trade – general background information about the slave trade was found in the large collection of appropriate references at the University of Birmingham library. There were two specific questions: were there any examples of Manx mariners being ill-treated by their captains and what really happened at the Massacre \at Old Calabar.

Sessional Papers: Minutes of Evidence
These Parliamentary records have been described as the best source of information about the Atlantic slave trade. There are two versions. The Abridged version, copies of which are held at Birmingham City Library, includes a description of the massacre at Old Calabar in 1767 but the full version is necessary for Ambrose Lace's evidence (se Chapter 9). This is held in the Abbot Papers, in the form of microprints at the University of Leicester.

No evidence was found of the ill-treatment of Manx mariners.

Table: Sources

Record & Archive Offices

Manx National Heritage Library	Customs Records
	Wills
	Atholl Papers
	Bridge House Papers
	Miscellaneous Papers
Public Record Office, Kew	Liverpool Port Books
	Port of Liverpool Muster Rolls
Cumbria Record Office	Walter Lutwidge Letterbooks
Denbighshire Record Office	William Boats's Will
	and general papers relating to his family
Lancashire Record Office	Wills of Manx People
Liverpool Record Office	Thomas Leyland Papers
	Tarleton Papers
	'Remarks on board the *Ranger*, John Corran'
	Letter of instruction for the *Blessing*, 1700
Carnegie Library, Ayr	Robert Arthur Letterbooks

Universities

Birmingham	Secondary Sources
Essex	Liverpool Trade & Shipping 1744 to 1786
Keele	William Davenport Papers
Leicester	Sessional Papers

Private Collection

Dalemain House	Christopher Hasell Papers

Footnotes

The abbreviations used in the footnotes are:

CRO: Cumbria Record Office
DRO: Denbighshire Record Office
MNHL: Manx National Heritage Library
LRO: Liverpool Record Office
PRO: Public Record Office, Kew

[1] MNHL 9707 AP40B-6 Representation: Commissioners, Customs, Scotland touching the Smuggling Trade from the Island of Man in a letter to Mr Whately June 7th 1764
[2] John J. McCusker, The current value of English exports 1697 to 1800 *William & Mary Quarterly* Third Series XXVIII 1971, pp 607-628
[3] William Davenport Papers. Keele Information Services – library. Keele University *William*: Captain William Patten, 23 November 1764.
[4] *Memoirs of the Late Captain Hugh Crow of Liverpool* 1830
[5] P.D. Richardson, *American Material from the Tarleton Papers in the Liverpool Record Office* British Records Relating to America in Microform 1974
[6] Encyclopaedia Britannica 1st edition 1771
[7] Joseph C. Miller, *Way of Death Merchant Capitalism and the Angolan Slave Trade 1730-1830* The University of Wisconsin Press 1988
[8] Gomer Williams, *History of the Liverpool Privateers with an account of the Liverpool Slave Trade* William Heinemann 1897 (see also note 130)
[9] MNHL 10058 The Charge of the Customs of Ingates & Outgates, Herring Customs, Wrecks etc. Ingates 1737
[10] LRO 387 MD42 Thomas Leyland & Co Account Book of the Ship *Lottery* to Captain Charles Kneale, Liverpool, 21 May 1802
[11] Marion Johnson, The Atlantic slave trade and the economy of West Africa in *Liverpool, the African Slave Trade, and Abolition* Edited by Roger Anstey & P.E.H. Hair Historic Society of Lancashire and Cheshire Occasional Series Volume 2 1976 p 18
[12] MNHL MS 501C (MIC 68) George Moore to Messrs Haliday & Dunbar, Liverpool, 7 February 1758 and 12 March 1759
[13] op cit George Moore to Thomas Rumbold, Liverpool, 26 May 1759
[14] MNHL 10058 Ingates & Outgates 1745
[15] PRO E190/1395/6 63253 Liverpool Port Books 1718
[16] D. Richardson, K. Beedham, M. M. Schofield, *Liverpool Trade and Shipping, 1744-1786* [computer file]. Colchester, Essex: The Data Archive [distributor], 27 July 1992. SN: 2923 – 54/81
[17] Arthur C. Wardle, Early Liverpool Vessels and Trade *The Mariner's Mirror* 25, 1939 pp 345-348
[18] Admiral W. H. Smith *Sailor's Word-book A Dictionary of Nautical Terms* 1867
[19] LRO NOR 2/179 Thomas Brownbell & John Murray, Gentleman, Captain and supercargo of the good ship *Blessing*, Liverpool, 10 August 1700
[20] MNHL 9707 APX11-38 Governor Lindsay to the Duke of Atholl, 30 October 1745
[21] PRO E190/1396/10 63253 Liverpool Port Books 1719
[22] PRO E190/1401/11 63253 Liverpool Port Books 1721
[23] LRO 920TAR2/8 Tarleton Papers
[24] MNHL 9707 APX35-2 Governor Cochrane to the Duke of Atholl, 18 February 1756
[25] David Richardson, The Eighteenth-Century British Slave Trade: Estimates of its volume and coastal distribution in Africa *Research in Economic History* 12 1989 pp 151-195
[26] MNHL 10071 Liber Canc 1760 f3 8 November 1759 & 6 December 1759
[27] William Davenport papers *Charming Nancy*: Samuel Sacheverell, 26 July 1753
[28] B. K. Drake The Liverpool-African voyage c. 1790-1807: commercial problems in *Liverpool, the African Slave Trade, and Abolition* Edited by Roger Anstey & P.E.H. Hair Historic Society of Lancashire and Cheshire Occasional Series Volume 2 1976 pp 126-156
[29] William Davenport papers *Charming Nancy*: Messrs Smith & Dowling, 9 October 1753

[30] William Davenport papers *Charming Nancy*: Samuel Sacheverell, 20 August 1754

[31] MNHL MS 501C (MIC 68) George Moore to Robert Kennish, Liverpool, 7 February 1759

[32] Act 7GeoICap20

[33] William Davenport papers *Charming Nancy*: Thomas Dickson, 23 March 1756

[34] Crosbie & Trafford, Wm. Rowe, Robert Green, Chas. Goore, Willm. Boats, Chas. Lowndes & Thos. Kelly to Captain Ambrose Lace, [of the *Marquis of Granby*] Liverpool, 14 April 1762 Gomer Williams: pp 486-488

[35] MNHL 10097 The Earle Family and Business Archive: Letter of instructions to William Earle, Captain of the *Chesterfield*, 1751

[36] MNHL 10071 Chancery File 1762

[37] MNHL F64 24XX The Report of the Commission of Inquiry for the Isle of Man 1792

[38] MNHL 9707 AP123-20 Memorandums taken by Captain Small relating to His Grace the Duke of Atholl's affairs in the Isle of Man

[39] PRONI T.1073/12 Continuation of transactions, correspondence by letters and occurrences to me, John Black, as are to be found in my pocket memorandum book begun since 1750. 23 & 24 September 1760

[40] MNHL 9707 APX17-16 Thomas Mears, Liverpool, to the Duke of Atholl, 3 September 1763

[41] Dalemain Archives. Christopher Hasell Papers. Letter Book 1. Christopher Hasell to Ned Hasell, Rotterdam, 13 May 1763 & Ned Hasell to Christopher Hasell, Liverpool, 3 May 1763

[42] MNHL 9707 APX8–25 John Tarleton, Liverpool, to the Duke of Atholl, 21 April 1759 & Duke of Atholl to John Tarleton, 4 May 1759

[43] MNHL 9707 APX8 (2nd)–13 George Baird, Glasgow, to the Duke of Atholl, 6 July 1759

[44] MNHL 9707 APX69(2nd)-22 Governor Cochrane to Duke of Atholl, 5 December 1757; AP Book 68 Duke of Atholl to Governor Cochrane, 23 November 1757, 25 February 1758, 18 May 1758 & 9 April 1759

[45] MNHL 9707 AP134 (4th)–13,14,15 Isle of Man: General abstract taken from Original Custom Books of India Goods brought from Liverpool etc From 10th October 1753 to 10th October 1763

[46] MNHL 9782 Castle Rushen Papers Document No. 77 1759 quoted in A365 1/7 The Journal of The Manx Museum Vol II No. 39 June 1934 p 187. Note: No original copy of this document could be found in the Castle Rushen papers in 1999

[47] Stephen D Behrendt *The British Slave Trade, 1785-1807: Volume, Profitability, and Mortality* PhD Thesis (unpublished) University of Wisconsin-Madison 1993

[48] MNHL MS 501C (MIC 68) George Moore to Messrs Haliday & Dunbar, Liverpool, 2 March 1759

[49] Based on Parliamentary Sessional Papers 1790: Minutes of Evidence before a Select Committee of the House of Commons appointed 29 January 1790

[50] PRO PROB11/1263 & DRO DD/DM/1325/42 Probate of the will (29 September 1793) of William Boates of Liverpool, merchant, 4 July 1795 [with previous will of 10 July 1792, and original will, 29 September 1793]

[51] MNHL 9707 APX8 (2nd)-23 Petition to James, Duke of Atholl, from Thomas Moore of Douglas, John Stevenson of Castletown and John Callin of Peeltown, 1 September 1759

[52] Frances Wilkins, *Walter Lutwidge, merchant of Whitehaven* in preparation

[53] Isle of Man Family History Society *Kirk German Parish Burial Register Book 1. 1665-1865* 1989

[54] Thomas M. Truxes, *Irish-American Trade 1660-1783* Cambridge University Press 1988

[55] Frances Wilkins, *The Isle of Man in Smuggling History* Wyre Forest Press 1992

[56] MNHL 9707 APX18-32 Memorial containing a relation of the Depredations and Irregular proceedings of George Dow commander of a cruiser sloop called the *Sincerity* belonging to the Custom Houses of Whitehaven and Liverpool, and other cruising vessels committed in and about the Isle of Man in the years 1748-1749 and 1750

[57] MNHL 9707 AP54-26 John Quayle to Duke of Atholl, 15 January 1751

[58] MNHL 9707 APX25-17 Governor Lindsay to the Duke of Atholl, 5 May 1747

[59] MNHL MS 501C (MIC 68) George Moore to Messrs Haliday & Dunbar, Liverpool, 5 January 1758

[60] MNHL 10071 Liber Canc 1755 f151, 1764 f22, 1766 f131

[61] MNHL 10058 Outgates 1714

[62] CRO Walter Lutwidge Letter Book Vol 1 & list printed in Edward Hughes *North Country Life in the Eighteenth Century Vol II: Cumberland & Westmoreland 1700-1830* OUP 1965

[63] David Richardson & M. M. Schofield Whitehaven and the eighteenth-century British Slave Trade *Transactions of the Cumberland and Westmorland Antiquarian and Archaeological Society* Vol XCII 1992 pp 183-204

[64] MNHL 9707 APX19(2nd)-27, 28, 31 Governor Lindsay to Duke of Atholl, 17 November 1750, Duke of Atholl to Governor Lindsay, 20 November 1750 & John Quayle to Duke of Atholl, 12 December 1756

[65] Frances Wilkins, *George Moore & Friends* Wyre Forest Press 1994

[66] MNHL MS 501C (MIC 68) George Moore to James Crosbie, Liverpool, 8 March 1753

[67] op cit George Moore to James Crosbie, Liverpool, 7 March 1751

[68] op cit George Moore to Messrs James & John Crosbie, Liverpool 24 December 1755

[69] MNHL 9707 APX69(2nd)-7 Memorial of Thomas Heywood of the Nunnery to Duke of Atholl, 5 September 1757

[70] MNHL 9707 AP Book 68 Duke of Atholl to Governor Cochrane, 18 September 1757

[71] MNHL 9782 Harbour Bundle 1757

[72] MNHL 9707 APX69(2nd)-12 Petition from Philip Moore and George Moore to Governor Cochrane, 24 October 1757

[73] MNHL 9707 APX69(2nd)–14 Francis Gildart Town Clerk, Liverpool, to Duke of Atholl, enclosing letter from the Mayor and merchants in Liverpool trading to foreign parts, 11 November 1757

[74] MNHL 9707 AP Book 68 Duke of Atholl to Francis Gildart, 23 November 1757

[75] MNHL 9707 APX69(2nd)-20 Statement from Commanders of Ships now in Douglas, 2 December 1757

[76] MNHL 9707 APX69(2nd)-22 Governor Cochrane to Duke of Atholl, 5 December 1757

[77] MNHL 9707 AP Book 68 Duke of Atholl to Governor Cochrane, 22 December 1757

[78] MNHL 9707 AP Book 68 Duke of Atholl to Francis Gildart, Town Clerk of Liverpool, 2 October 1758

[79] MNHL 9707 APX46-15 George Moore to Duke of Atholl, 20 February 1759

[80] MNHL MS 501C (MIC 68) George Moore to Messrs Haliday & Dunbar, Liverpool, 5 January 1758

[81] op cit George Moore to James Gildart, Liverpool, 2 March 1759

[82] op cit George Moore to Messrs Haliday & Dunbar, Liverpool 2 March & 5 April 1759

[83] op cit George Moore to Thomas Rumbold, Liverpool, 26 May 1759

[84] MNHL 9707 APX46-27 Memorial of George Moore & Thomas Mylrae, supervisors of the harbour of Peeltown, 20 April 1759

[85] MNHL MS 501C (MIC 68) George Moore to Haliday & Dunbar, Liverpool 2 March 1759

[86] op cit George Moore to Haliday & Dunbar 5 April 1759

[87] op cit George Moore to John Maine, Liverpool, 24 November 1758

[88] MNHL 9707 APX46-15 George Moore to Duke of Atholl, 20 February 1759

[89] MNHL 9707 AP145-24 Memorial from the inhabitants of Peel & its vicinity to Duke of Atholl, 23 July 1799

[90] IoMNHAS Vol 4 No. 4 p 516 – source the Internet

[91] MNHL 9707 APX5-29 Hugh Cosnahan to George Farquhar, Edinburgh, 2 May 1789

[92] MNHL 9707 APX28-20 Governor Cochrane to Duke of Atholl, 18 September 1756

[93] Frances Wilkins, *The Running Trade*, in preparation

[94] David Hancock, *Citizens of the World London merchants and the integration of the British Atlantic community, 1735-1785* Cambridge University Press 1995

[95] LRO 920TAR2/4; 920TAR2/6; 920TAR2/10; 920TAR2/11 Tarleton Papers

[96] Carnegie Library, Ayr, Letter Books of Robert Arthur, merchant in Irvine. Robert Arthur to James Oates, Douglas, 6 February 1765

[97] Dalemain Archives Christopher Hasell Papers Letter Book 2. Christopher Hasell to Mark Nesfield at the Powder Office in Broad Street, London 18 May 1765; 20 July 1765; 5 March 1766; 20 April 1766; 7 June 1766; 30 September 1766; 28 June 1766; 7 November 1766; 7 November 1766; 22 November 1767

[98] MNHL 9707 AP Book 70 Minutes of Evidence No. 11 The Examination of Mr Hugh Cosnahan, taken at Douglas in the Isle of Man, 27 September 1791

[99] MNHL 9707 AP36/38(2nd)-6 Hugh Cosnahan to Duke of Atholl, 1 November 1765

[100] MNHL 9707 AP33B-30 Daniel Mylrae & John Quayle to Duke of Atholl, 10 April 1766

[101] MNHL 9707 AP33B-18 John Taubman to Dan Mylrae & John Quayle, 22 July 1765

[102] MNHL 9707 AP33B-32 Daniel Mylrae & John Quayle to Duke of Atholl n.d.

[103] MNHL BH3526 Hugh Cosnahan to George Moore, 10 July 1776

[104] MNHL BH3550 Hugh Cosnahan to George Moore, 26 February 1783

[105] MNHLBH3553 Hugh Cosnahan to George Moore, 4 March 1783

[106] MNHL BH3554 Hugh Cosnahan to George Moore, 10 March 1783

[107] MNHL BH3556 James Oates to Hugh Cosnahan, 11 April 1783

[108] MNHL 9707 APX5-29 Hugh Cosnahan to George Farquhar, Edinburgh, 2 May 1789

[109] MNHL 9707 APX5-30 Hugh Cosnahan to George Farquhar, Edinburgh, 31 May 1789

[110] MNHL 9707 AP5-36 Hugh Cosnahan to George Farquhar, Edinburgh, 7 April 1790

[111] MNHL 9707 APX28-32 Basil Cochrane to Duke of Atholl, 9 December 1756

[112] Walter E. Minchinton Characteristics of British Slaving Vessels 1698-1775 *Journal of Interdisciplinary History* XX:1 (Summer 1989) pp 53-81

[113] MNHL 9707 APX17-15 David Ross, Robert Mercer, Thomas Gillespie, Robert Gordon & William McCall to Duke of Atholl, 26 August 1763

[114] MNHL 9707 AP44B-28 Petition & memorial of the principal merchants and traders within the Isle of Man to Duke and Duchess of Atholl, n.d.

[115] William Davenport papers. Waste Book 6 October 1760 and 13 November 1760

[116] Carnegie Library, Ayr, Letters Books of Robert Arthur, merchant in Irvine. Robert Arthur to James Montgomerie of the *Kennedy* at Belfast 13 September 1768

[117] David Richardson Profit in the Liverpool slave trade: the accounts of William Davenport, 1757-1784 in *Liverpool, the African Slave Trade, and Abolition* Edited by Roger Anstey & P.E.H. Hair Historic Society of Lancashire and Cheshire Occasional Series Volume 2 1976 pp 60-90

[118] Dalemain Archives. Christopher Hasell Papers. Letter Book 2. Christopher Hasell to Mark Nesfield, 7 November 1766 and 26 December 1766

[119] John Newton *The Journal of a Slave Trader 1750-1754* with Newton's Thoughts upon the African Slave Trade edited, with an introduction, by Bernard Martin and Mark Spurrell The Epworth Press London 1962

[120] LRO 387MD43 Thomas Leyland & Co Account Book of the ship Enterprise to Captain Caesar Lawson, 18 July 1803

[121] A.W. Moore *Manx Worthies* 1901 p 176

[122] LRO 387MD56 Remarks on board the brig *Ranger* John Corran

[123] The Book of Common Prayer: To be used at sea: Thanksgiving after a storm

[124] Stephen D. Behrendt *The British Slave Trade, 1785-1807: Volume, Profitability, and Mortality* Unpublished PhD Thesis University of Wisconsin-Madison 1993 p 123

[125] William Davenport papers. Waste Book 13 February 1751

[126] British Sessional Papers 1731-1800 House of Commons. Accounts & Papers Vol. 29 1790

[127] David Richardson *Bristol, Africa and the Eighteenth-Century Slave Trade to America Vol. 3 The Years of Decline 1746-1769.* Bristol Record Society's Publications 1991 1767/8, 1767/11 & 1767/19

[128] Elizabeth Donnan Documents Illustrative of the Slave Trade to America Volume 11 The Eighteenth Century Carnegie Institution 1931 p 533

[129] Gomer Williams. Ambrose lace to Thomas Jones, Bristol, 11 November 1773 pp 541-542

[130] Gomer Williams. Letters to Ambrose Lace pp 542-549

[131] Dalemain Archives. Christopher Hasell papers. No. 26 *True Blue*, Joshua Hatton captain, crew list and contract, 2 August 1768

[132] PRO BT98/65 Port of Liverpool. Muster roll of the ship *Ceres*, Adam Elliott master, 3 September 1805

[133] MNHL 10071 Liber Scac 1736-1742 Presentments 1736

[134] op cit Petition of William Kneen approved by Governor Murray 30 March 1738

[135] MNHL 9381 Copy of a Document written by Charles Christian, giving some episodes of his life

[136] PRO BT98/61 Port of Liverpool. Muster roll for the ship *Will*, Hugh Crow master, 2 October 1801

[137] MNHL 10071 Liber Causarum 1774

[138] J. C. Willis *A Dictionary of the Flowering Plants and Ferns.* Cambridge 1948

[139] A. W. Moore *Manx Worthies* 1901 pp 175-176

[140] Stephen D. Behrendt The Captains in the British Slave Trade from 1785 to 1807 *Transactions of the Historic Society of Lancashire and Cheshire* 140 1990 pp 79-140

[141] MNHL A365 1/7 Ann Harrison The Mathematical School, Peel *The Journal of the Manx Museum* Vol. 7 Issue 88 1976 pp 212-216 including Plate 53

[142] PRO BT98/64 Port of Liverpool Muster roll for the ship *Jane* Quayle Fargher master, 27 March 1787

[143] Suzanne Schwartz *Slave Captain The Career of James Irving in the Liverpool Slave Trade* Edited with Introduction Bridge House Books, Wrexham, Clawed 1995

[144] PRO BT98/51 No. 248 Port of Liverpool Muster roll for the ship *Diana* & email from Stephen Behrendt dated 5 August 1999

[145] PRO BT98/60 Port of Liverpool Muster roll for the *Charlotte* William Crow & Chambers Reed, 6 November 1800

[146] Williamson's Liverpool Advertiser No 262 29 May 1761

[147] PRO BT98/59 Port of Liverpool Muster for the *Triton* John Corran and Francis Stowell, 10 January 1799

[148] MNHL 9709 AP108(2nd)-40 J Cosnahan to the Duke of Atholl, 19 March 1817

[149] Lancashire RO WCW Philip Kewley 1792

[150] Williamsons Liverpool Advertiser 3 July & 10 July 1761

[151] Lancashire RO WCW Robert Waterson 1766

[152] Lancashire RO WCW Hugh Kissack 1800

[153] MNHL MS 5511C, MS 5513C, MS5514C & MS5515C assorted papers relating to Quayle Fargher

[154] MNHL L9/J1 Jefferson's Manks Almanack 1808

[155] PRO BT98/50 Port of Liverpool Muster roll for the brig *Ranger* John Corran master, 9 December 1790

[156] LRO 387MD43 Thomas Leyland & Co Account Book of the ship *Enterprize* to Captain Caesar Lawson, 18 July 1803

[157] Lancashire RO WCW John Corran 1822

[158] James A. Rawley *The Transatlantic Slave Trade: A History* Norton & Co London, New York 1981

[159] PRO BT98/68 Port of Liverpool Muster roll for the *Kitty's Amelia* Hugh Crow, 13 August 1808

[160] PRO BT98/61Port of Liverpool Muster roll for the ship *William*, Richard Hart master 2 January 1801

[161] PRO BT98/64 Port of Liverpool Muster roll for the *Dart* Edward Crosby master, 21 June 1804

[162] PRO BT98/64 Port of Liverpool muster roll for the *Dick* Captain George Irvin master, 5 July 1804

Index